Start Smart

BUILDING BRAIN POWER IN THE EARLY YEARS, REVISED

by Pam Schiller

ALSO BY PAM SCHILLER

The Bilingual Book of Rhymes, Songs, Stories, and Fingerplays, with Rafael Lara-Alecio and Beverly J. Irby

Bountiful Earth

Bugs, Bugs, Bugs

The Complete Resource Book for Infants

The Complete Resource Book for Preschoolers

The Complete Resource Book for Toddlers and Twos

The Complete Book of Rhymes, Songs, Poems, Fingerplays, and Chants, with Jackie Silberg

The Complete Book of Activities, Games, Stories, Props, Recipes, and Dances, with Jackie Silberg

Count on Math, with Lynne Peterson

Creating Readers

Critters and Company

Do You Know the Muffin Man? with Thomas Moore

Fabulous Food

Honk, Honk, Rattle, Rattle

The Instant Curriculum, Revised, with Joan Rosanno

Me, My Family, and Friends

The Practical Guide to Quality Child Care, with Patricia Carter Dyke

School Days

Seven Skills for School Success

The Values Book, with Tamera Bryant

Where Is Thumbkin? with Thomas Moore

Wild, Wild West

A PAM SCHILLER BOOK

Start Smart

Revised Edition

BUILDING BRAIN POWER IN THE EARLY YEARS

direct experience

trial and error

active exploration

repetition

Gryphon House, Inc.
P.O. Box 10, 6848 Leon's Way
Lewisville, North Carolina, USA

Pam Schiller
Illustrated by Deb Johnson

Library of Congress Cataloging-in-Publication Information

Schiller, Pamela Byrne
  Start smart! : building brain power in the early years / Pam Schiller. -- 2nd ed.
      p. cm.
   ISBN 978-0-87659-393-6 (pbk.)
   1. Ability in children. 2. Intellect--Problems, exercises, etc. 3. Learning, Psychology of--Problems, exercises, etc. 4. Child psychology. I. Title.
   BF723.A25S35 2012
   649'.123--dc23

                                        2011049685

Bulk purchase

Gryphon House books are available for special premiums and sales promotions as well as for fund-raising use. Special editions or book excerpts also can be created to specification. For details, contact the Director of Marketing at Gryphon House.

Disclaimer

Gryphon House, Inc., and the author cannot be held responsible for damage, mishap, or injury incurred during the use of or because of activities in this book. Appropriate and reasonable caution and adult supervision of children involved in activities and corresponding to the age and capability of each child are recommended at all times. Do not leave children unattended at any time. Observe safety and caution at all times.

Table of Contents

Introduction 7

CHAPTER 1
Sniff, Sniff:
Aromas and the Brain 15

CHAPTER 2
Thinking It Through:
Choices and the Brain 21

CHAPTER 3
I Feel Blue: Color and the Brain.....25

CHAPTER 4
Always Across: Cross-Lateral
Movement and the Brain.................31

CHAPTER 5
I Feel, I Remember:
Emotions and the Brain...................41

CHAPTER 6
Hop, Skip, Jump:
Exercise and the Brain 49

CHAPTER 7
Right and Left:
Hemispheres and the Brain 55

CHAPTER 8
Water, Water, Everywhere:
Hydration and the Brain 59

CHAPTER 9
Laughter and Learning:
Laughter and the Brain...................65

CHAPTER 10
I Hear! I See! I Do!
Learning Styles and the Brain 71

CHAPTER 11
Touch, Toss, Turn, Twirl:
Movement and the Brain.................75

CHAPTER 12
Start with a Song:
Music and the Brain 81

CHAPTER 13
The Power of New:
Novelty and the Brain 89

CHAPTER 14
Feeding the Brain:
Nutrition and the Brain...................95

CHAPTER 15
Less Is More!
Overstimulation and the Brain....101

CHAPTER 16
More than Plaids:
Patterns and the Brain 107

CHAPTER 17
Try, Try, Again:
Practice and the Brain 115

CHAPTER 18
Solving Problems:
Problem Solving and the Brain....119

CHAPTER 19
Praise or Encouragement:
Rewards, Praise, and the Brain ...129

CHAPTER 20
Spanish, Japanese, Vietnamese:
Second Language Learning
and the Brain 133

CHAPTER 21
What Does It Mean? Sense, Meaning,
and the Brain 141

CHAPTER 22
The Hand-Brain Connection:
Small Muscles and the Brain........145

CHAPTER 23
Calm, Cool, and Collected?
Stress and the Brain 153

CHAPTER 24
The Good, the Bad, and the
Unknown: Technology and
the Brain...159

Glossary...163

Appendix 168

Index...173

Introduction

When old ideas, assumptions, and theories converge with new ideas, needs, insights, and technologies, we have an opportunity to move forward in our thinking. Because of research in brain development, we know more than we did before about how to offer children the best possible foundation for learning. *Start Smart: Building Brain Power in the Early Years,* Revised is filled with both information and ideas that translate brain research to practical, easy-to-do activities for young children.

The human brain may only weigh three pounds, but those three pounds are some of the most fascinating on this planet—possibly in the universe. Although often compared to a computer, the human brain is far more complex and far more capable. In fact, the human brain takes in and organizes more information in a day than a computer is capable of processing in years. Researchers estimate that the human brain receives between 35,000 and 40,000 bits of information per second. Of course, much of this information is screened out, or our brains would blow the equivalent of a fuse.

The human brain is capable of imagining and creating the spaceship that took us to the moon, laser surgery, video and computer games, baseball, the automobile, the computer, Mozart's "Requiem Mass," Leonardo da Vinci's "Mona Lisa," electricity, spaghetti, and building blocks—all of this from an organ that is about the size of a grapefruit.

Long before birth, the brain begins building the neural connections for everything—from breathing and sight to the ability to speak, think, and reason. Although the structure is in place, it will be up to the environment to strengthen and "grow" the pathways. Neuroscience research supports the idea that the environment is ultimately responsible for who we turn out to be (Goleman, 2005; Gordon & Lemons, 1997). Nature endows us with inborn abilities and traits; nurture takes these genetic tendencies and molds them as we learn and mature. This view of the nature-versus-nurture debate is referred to as the interactive perspective (Gordon & Lemons, 1997).

Start Smart: Building Brain Power in the Early Years, Revised focuses on the key findings of brain research, exploring how and when we can strengthen brain connections. This book also explores environmental influences that enhance brain functions and provides strategies to help optimize learning.

FIVE KEY FINDINGS ON BRAIN DEVELOPMENT

When current brain research is summarized, what emerges are simple, easy-to-understand findings that, for the most part, reinforce what we know intuitively. The following is a list of the five most relevant findings:

- **Brain development is contingent upon a complex interplay between genes and environment.** There is currently little debate about whether learning is more dependent upon nature or nurture. It is clear from the research that nature lays down a complex system of brain circuitry, but how that circuitry is "wired" depends upon external forces such as nutrition, surroundings, and stimulation. Daniel Goleman (2006) estimates that 70 percent of who we turn out to be is a product of the experiences we encounter in our environment.

  - **Early experiences contribute significantly to the structure of the brain and its capacities.** The quality, quantity, consistency, and timing of stimulation will determine, to a large extent, the number of brain synapses that form and how those connections function. This is true for all areas of development (cognitive, physical, social, emotional, and linguistic), and the effect is lifelong.

□ **Early interactions are critical to brain structure.** Children learn in the context of important relationships. Brain-cell connections are established as children experience the surrounding world and form attachments to parents, family members, and caregivers. Warm, responsive care appears to have a protective biological function, helping children weather ordinary stresses and prepare for the adverse effects of later stress or trauma. Nonresponsive care, absence of care, drug abuse, and trauma can all have an adverse effect on children's emotional well-being. During the first four months of life, spindle cells, which are related to the development of social judgment and sensitivity, position themselves in the brain. How freely spindle cells grow depends on factors such as stress (fewer spindle cells) and loving atmosphere (more spindle cells) (Goleman, 2005). During the first two years of life, mirror cells develop and connect. These cells are also dependent on positive human interactions. Mirror cells are directly related to children's later capacity for empathy (Goleman, 2005).

□ **Brain development is nonlinear.** Learning continues across the life cycle; however, there are windows of opportunity during which the brain is particularly efficient at specific types of learning. Certain critical periods are conducive to developing specific skills. For example, children are most receptive to second-language learning from birth to ten. Children are particularly in tune with music between the ages of three and ten. Brain development is not a step-by-step process; it is more like a spiral with waves or windows of opportunity. The order of the windows listed in the chart below is chronological. They are the same for all children no matter where or under what conditions they are born.

Windows of Opportunity*

Window	Wiring Opportunity	Greatest Enhancement

Emotional Intelligence
  Trust
  Impulse Control
	0–48 months
	0–14 months
	16–48 months
		4 years to puberty

Social Development
  Attachment
  Independence
  Cooperation
	0–48 months
	0–12 months
	18–36 months
	24–48 months
		4 years to puberty

Thinking Skills
  Cause and Effect
  Problem Solving
	0–48 months
	0–16 months
	16–48 months
		4 years to puberty

Motor Development	0–24 months	2 years to puberty
Vision	0–24 months	2 years to puberty

Language
  Early Sounds
  Vocabulary
	0–24 months
	4–8 months
	0–24 months
		2–7 years
		8 months to puberty
		2–5 years

+Second Languages
  Vocabulary
  Formal Instruction
	0–60 months (sounds)
	0–10 years (syntax)	

*Windows of opportunity are difficult to pinpoint because results from different studies differ slightly. The windows in this chart are based on the most frequently quoted data. The second column (Wiring Opportunity) refers to when the brain is most receptive to wiring. The third column (Greatest Enhancement) refers to opportunities for strengthening the wiring. The windows are open until puberty for most individuals. If skills are not wired within the wiring opportunity time frame, they can still be wired up to puberty. However, skills not wired within a designated wiring window will not wire to the optimum level that could have been achieved (Ramey & Ramey, 1996). The farther past a window a child is when intervention occurs, the less likely that child's brain will wire to develop that skill.

+ Researchers have come to varying conclusions regarding second-language acquisition. From birth to age five is when a second language is easiest for children to acquire, and if children are exposed to two languages that are spoken by native speakers during this time, children should be able to acquire and speak both languages fluently. However, some believe that children are better off mastering their native language before being introduced to a second language. Others suggest offering children up to age five a 50-word vocabulary in a second language and then beginning formal instruction between the ages of five and 10.

☐ **Children are biologically prepared to learn.** The brain of a three-year-old is two-and-a-half times more active than that of an adult. Children's brains have more synapses than adult brains and the density of synapses remains high throughout the first 10 years of life.

WHAT IS NEUROSCIENCE?

Neuroscience research studies how the brain works. Until 1980, information about the brain could only be obtained through animal studies and human autopsies. In the last decades, technological advances have provided noninvasive ways for scientists to study the brains of living people. These advances have provided researchers with a more sophisticated understanding of the brain's function.

Using imaging tools—Ultrasound, CAT, MRI, MEG, NIRS, fMRI, PET, and EEG— scientists can study brain function, structure, and energy. The information gained through these tools has changed forever the way we view the human capacity for learning. We have broadened our perspective from a purely psychological base of understanding (grounded in the theories of Piaget, Skinner, and Maslow) to one that includes a biological (science-driven) base of understanding. The combination of psychology and biology has provided new insight into how children and adults access and remember information, and has given us new ways to view intelligence.

NEURAL NETWORKS

The human brain is made up of tens of millions of neural networks that function simultaneously in interconnected combinations.

According to Robert Sylwester (2010), if a person observes a red ball rolling along a table, that person's brain processes the color, shape, movement, and location of the ball in four separate brain areas. Despite the debates about left and right hemispheres and how special areas of the brain relate to multiple intelligences, the brain functions as an integrated whole and is responsible for actions, emotions, and thoughts.

Indications are that we have the period from birth to approximately age 10 to help children develop the "wiring" of the brain. The more one reads about brain research, the clearer it is that the key to intelligence is the recognition of patterns and relationships in all that we experience. Strengthening children's neural networks then becomes the job of helping children develop an awareness of patterns and relationships, and guiding children to make connections between these known patterns and relationships to new information.

BRAIN FUNCTIONS

The human brain is constantly collecting information from the environment—an average of 40,000 stimuli per second. We obtain about 95 percent of this information through the senses of vision, touch, and hearing. All of this information enters our short-term memory at an unconscious level. Because it is impossible for the brain to pay attention to this many pieces of information at one time, it begins a screening process, seeking what is relevant and registering only the information that matches the individual's experiences.

THE HUMAN BRAIN COLLECTS AN AVERAGE OF 40,000 STIMULI PER SECOND.

The filtered information is passed on to the brain's working memory (still short-term). It is here that the brain focuses and gives its conscious attention to the information for the first time as the brain attempts to make sense of the information and establish meaning for it. If the brain is able to connect the new information with existing information, the brain will store that information in its long-term memory.

Memory refers to the process by which the brain retains mental impressions or knowledge and skills. The brain has a virtually unlimited capacity to store information in its memory. When the brain encounters new learning, it goes through both physical and chemical changes. This process helps form new neural networks and reinforce established networks.

Retention refers to the process whereby long-term memory preserves learning in such a way that the brain can locate, identify, and retrieve that information accurately in the future.

USING THIS BOOK

Misinterpretations of neuroscience information are often portrayed in television commercials and magazine advertisements. You see and hear slogans about products that claim to increase brain power. Families buy flashcards for babies, enroll very young children in music lessons, or wonder if they should reorganize their finances to allow one parent to stay at home. This book is designed to show how to use brain research to build a foundation for future learning, not to encourage a push for early learning. Children need what they have always needed—warm, loving, and responsive parents and caregivers; an interesting and safe environment to explore; healthy food and good medical care; and other children to play with. Brain research helps us identify what young children need so that they develop the greatest capacity for learning and living.

Start Smart: Building Brain Power in the Early Years, Revised is a collection of scientific findings and activities that appropriately apply brain research information to everyday experiences. Beneath the umbrella of the five key findings are literally hundreds of research results that have a direct impact on our understanding of how children's brains develop and that show us how to enhance children's learning opportunities.

This book takes some of these findings, explains how they affect children, and then offers suggestions for applying this information. A list of suggested children's books and a bibliography of books for more in-depth reading are provided for each chapter.

Each day approximately 490,000 babies are born. That means we have 490,000 new opportunities daily to help children forge and strengthen brain connections. What are we waiting for? Our generation is the first to be armed with the scientific knowledge of "how." Let's not miss our window of opportunity.

Want to Read More?

Goleman, D. 2006. *Social intelligence: The new science of human relationships.* New York: Bantam.

Gordon, E. & Lemons, M. 1997. An interactionist perspective on the genesis of intelligence, in Robert J. Sternberg and Elena Grigorenko, eds. *Intelligence, heredity, and the environment.* Cambridge, UK: Cambridge University Press.

Ramey, C. & Ramey, S. 1999. *Right from birth: Building your child's foundation for life.* New York: Goddard Press.

Shore, R. 2003. *Rethinking the brain,* revised. Washington, DC: Families and Work Institute.

Sousa, D. 2005. *How the brain learns.* New York: Corwin Press.

Sylwester, R. 2010. *A child's brain: The need for nurture.* New York: Corwin Press.

Sniff, Sniff!

AROMAS AND THE BRAIN

Our sense of smell is the only sense that sends information directly to the brain. Of the 12 nerve endings that enter the brain, only the olfactory (sense of smell) passes stimuli to the brain unfiltered. Our sense of smell affects our brain chemistry and changes our moods in powerful ways. Researchers have found that certain odors increase the ability to learn, create, and think. Other aromas are thought to boost attention and learning. Peppermint, basil, lemon, cinnamon, and rosemary are linked to mental alertness. Lavender, chamomile, orange, and rose promote relaxation and calming. Certain types of scent stimulation, like the smell of food, can disrupt the learning functions of our brain. Chemical smells from air fresheners, perfume, and even some essential oils can be distracting and can block learning.

The chart below shows some common conditions and the aromas that may help improve these conditions.

Condition	Effective Herb*
Low energy	Basil, cinnamon, clove, garlic, geranium, hyssop, marjoram, nutmeg, pine
Anxiety	Basil, chamomile, eucalyptus, jasmine, marjoram, neroli, rose, thyme, ylang-ylang
Depression	Borneo camphor, chamomile, jasmine, lavender, nutmeg, thyme, verbena
Irritability	Chamomile, cypress, jasmine, lavender, marjoram, melissa, nutmeg, rose, vanilla, verbena
Stress/Fatigue	Basil, chamomile, cinnamon, clove, cypress, frankincense, jasmine, lavender, marjoram, neroli, orange, rose, sage, savory, sandalwood, thyme, vanilla, verbena

*Check for allergies to herbs and spices.

Scents have a strong association with memory. Has it ever happened that when you smell an aroma you suddenly remember an event that you had forgotten, or that the smell of cologne reminds you of a particular person? These are examples of the connection between the sense of smell (olfaction) and memory.

The primary olfactory cortex, where processing of olfactory information takes place, forms a direct link with the amygdala and the hippocampus. Only two synapses separate the olfactory nerve from the amygdala, which is the part of the brain where emotion is experienced and remembered. Only three synapses separate the olfactory nerve from the hippocampus, which is critical to forming memory, especially working memory and short-term memory. The sense of smell is the sensory modality that is physically closest to the limbic system, of which the hippocampus and amygdala are a part, and which is responsible for emotions and memory. Researchers believe this may be why odor-evoked memories are often emotionally potent (Herz & Engen, 1996).

Ideas for Using Aromas to Enhance Children's Attention

Experiences and Activities for Infants and Toddlers

☐ Use mint-scented soaps in the morning to increase alertness, and lavender-scented soaps later in the day for restfulness.

☐ Place an article of Mom's clothing in the crib. The familiar smell will calm the baby. Babies can recognize their mother by smell during the first week of life (Ramey & Ramey, 1999)

☐ Make nontoxic playdough for toddlers using one of the following recipes. Check for allergies before using.

RECIPE CARD

Gelatin Playdough

1 cup flour
½ cup salt
1 cup water
1 tablespoon cooking oil
2 teaspoons cream of tartar
1 (3½ ounce) package plain, unsweetened gelatin
vanilla extract (or another extract)
Equipment: saucepan, measuring cups and spoons, mixing spoon, airtight container

Mix all ingredients together and cook over medium heat, stirring constantly until mixture is the consistency of mashed potatoes. Let cool and knead with floured hands until dry. Cool completely before storing in airtight container.

Start Smart, Revised

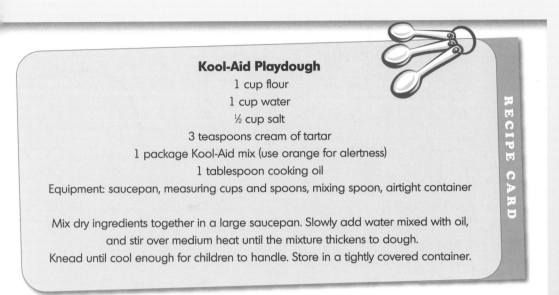

Kool-Aid Playdough

1 cup flour

1 cup water

½ cup salt

3 teaspoons cream of tartar

1 package Kool-Aid mix (use orange for alertness)

1 tablespoon cooking oil

Equipment: saucepan, measuring cups and spoons, mixing spoon, airtight container

Mix dry ingredients together in a large saucepan. Slowly add water mixed with oil, and stir over medium heat until the mixture thickens to dough. Knead until cool enough for children to handle. Store in a tightly covered container.

Experiences and Activities for Preschool Children

☐ Design cooking activities that will release aromas that increase alertness. For example, cinnamon rolls have an aroma that encourages mental alertness.

Cinnamon Rolls

2 cups baking mix, such as Bisquick

⅔ cup milk

¼ cup sugar

margarine or butter

1 teaspoon ground cinnamon

Equipment: cookie sheet, 2 small bowls, rolling pin, measuring cups and spoons, table knife, breadboard, fork, oven

Combine baking mix and milk in a small bowl and beat with a fork. Place dough on a floured surface and knead gently. Roll the dough into an 8" x 12" rectangle and spread with margarine. Mix sugar and cinnamon in another bowl and sprinkle it over the dough. Roll the dough tightly and pinch its ends closed. Cut the roll into 1" slices and place them on a greased cookie sheet. Bake 15 minutes at 425° F.

☐ Use scented playdough. Substituting three tablespoons of massage oil for the vegetable oil suggested in most playdough recipes makes great scented playdough (see Scented Playdough Recipe #1). Flavored powdered drink mix, such as Kool-Aid, also creates a nicely scented playdough (see Scented Playdough Recipe #2).

RECIPE CARD

Scented Playdough Recipe #1

3 cups flour

1½ cups salt

3 tablespoons massage oil

2 tablespoons cream of tartar

3 cups water

Equipment: measuring cups and spoons, saucepan, mixing spoon, stove or hot plate

Combine all ingredients in a saucepan and cook over very low heat until mixture is no longer sticky to the touch.

RECIPE CARD

Scented Playdough Recipe #2

1 package powdered drink mix, such as Kool-Aid

1 cup water

1 teaspoon baby oil

1 cup flour

½ cup salt

2 teaspoons cream of tartar

Equipment: measuring cups and spoons, saucepan, mixing spoon, stove or hot plate, wax paper

Stir the drink mix and water in a saucepan over medium heat until steam rises. Add baby oil and stir. Mix together the remaining dry ingredients. Gradually add the dry mixture to the heated liquids and stir until a mashed-potato consistency is achieved. Remove from stove; place playdough on wax paper and knead until smooth. Allow to cool. Have fun!

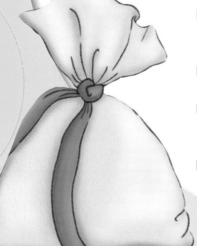

- ☐ Provide scented markers for children to use for writing and drawing activities. Create your own scented markers by dipping dried-up markers in scented dyes or paints.
- ☐ Add cooking extracts or massage oils to tempera paint, then ask the children to make "scent-sational" paintings.
- ☐ Use potpourri. Children can make their own by placing cloves, cinnamon sticks, or scented cotton balls in a 4" square of netting, then tying it closed with a piece of ribbon.
- ☐ Provide hand lotion by the sink for children to use after washing their hands.

- Make scratch-and-sniff pictures. Mix gelatin using only half the amount of water called for in the recipe. Let the children use this mixture as paint. After the paint dries, the children can scratch and sniff their artwork.
- Make perfume. Collect old flowers from a florist. Remove the petals and place them in a large, empty can. Add enough water to cover the petals. Put the can in a saucepan of water, and heat on low heat for a couple of hours (an adult-only step). Strain the liquid to use as perfume.
- Grow an herb garden. Introduce children to various herbs, and invite the children to participate in cooking activities that use the herbs.
- Fill beanbags with herbs. Encourage children to play games with the beanbags.
- Take a nature walk. Encourage children to close their eyes and try to identify the smells of nature.
- Place calming or relaxing aromas in quiet areas, and aromas that encourage alertness in more active areas.
- Make smelling bottles by dipping cotton balls in extracts and placing them in small plastic containers. Poke holes in the lids (an adult-only step). Create two of each scent, and encourage children to match the scents by using their sense of smell.
- Create scented crayons for children to use. Melt old and broken crayons in muffin tins on a warming tray. Add oil-based extracts before the wax hardens.
- Keep fresh flowers in the room.

Experiences and Activities for School-Age Children
- Keep scented items (lemon or orange peel, perfume, cedar, pine needles, coffee, vinegar, chocolate, or any other scent) separated and enclosed in plastic containers so that the odors do not mix. Punch holes in the tops of the containers (an adult-only step). Ask the children to identify each smell, describe its odor (pleasant, unpleasant, strong, mild) and then encourage the children to talk about any memories they associate with the smells.
- Make collections of seriated scents. Place a single scent (cologne, fruit juice, extracts) in four plastic containers. Add different amounts of water to each container so that the scent is more and more diluted. Mark the order of dilution on the bottoms of the containers. Mix the containers and then ask children to arrange the containers from strongest to weakest scent. If the children place the containers in the incorrect order, help the

children identify at which point they made mistakes. If they try the activity with another scent, do they make similar mistakes? Do the children improve their ability to place the containers in the correct order as they repeat the activity?

☐ Invite children to make perfume. Place cut flower petals (lavender, lilac, honeysuckle, gardenias) in a cup of water. Cover the bowl with plastic wrap and let stand it overnight. Strain the mixture through cheesecloth (or a coffee filter) into a small bottle. Encourage children to describe the scent of their perfume, and ask them to describe any memories the scent might trigger.

Books for Infants and Toddlers

Little Bunny Follows His Nose by Katherine Howard
Sniff, Sniff: A Book About Smell by Dana Meachen

Books for Preschool Children

Smelling Things by Allen Fowler
Nose Book by Al Perkins
Sniffing and Smelling by Henry Arthur Pluckrose

Smell by Kay Woodward
Smelling by Richard L. Allington

Books for School-Age Children

Nate the Great and the Big Sniff by Marjorie Weinman Sharmat
The Nose Knows by Avery Gilbert
Stink and the World's Worst Super-Stinky Sneakers by Megan McDonald

Want to Read More?

Gottfried, J. A., Smith, A. P. R., Rugg, M. D. & Dolan, R. J. 2004. Remembrance of odors past: Human olfactory cortex in crossmodal recognition memory. *Neuron*, 42: 687–695.

Herz R. S. & Engen T. 1996. Odor memory: Review and analysis. *Psychonomic bulletin and review* 3: n3 300–313.

Ramey, C. & Ramey, S. 1999. *Right from birth: Building your child's foundation for life.* New York: Goddard Press.

Sullivan, R. M., McGaugh, J. L., & Leon, M. 1999. Norepinphrine-induced plasticity and one-trial olfactory learning in neonatal rats. *Brain Research* 60.2: 219-28.

Thinking It Through

CHOICES AND THE BRAIN

When children have the freedom to make choices, especially about learning activities, they feel more positive about their work, and at the same time, they feel less anxiety. High anxiety causes the release of hormones that inhibit learning, while low anxiety enhances the ability to learn. Positive feelings trigger the release of endorphins, which enhance the functioning of brain connections. Having the freedom to make choices allows learners to reach self-determined goals, sparking and maintaining motivation, which is critical to learning.

Although offering choices enhances learning, children do not make thoughtful choices when they are presented with more than three options (Jensen, 2008). Toddlers are typically only able to handle two options thoughtfully. Too many choices overwhelm children (and their brains). Adults typically can consider no more than six options at one time.

ALTHOUGH OFFERING CHOICES ENHANCES LEARNING, CHILDREN DO NOT MAKE THOUGHTFUL

CHOICES WHEN THEY ARE PRESENTED WITH MORE THAN THREE OPTIONS (JENSEN, 2008).

Ideas for Using Choice to Increase Motivation

Experiences and Activities for Infants and Toddlers

▢ Offer children six months or older two choices. Describe each option using a simple sentence.

▢ Place two toys close to the child so he can choose the toy he wants to play with.

▢ Discuss the choices you make for children. For example, *I am going to sit you next to Quinn today. Yesterday you sat by Audrey.*

▢ Use choices as often as possible when soliciting children's cooperation. For example, *Would you prefer water or milk?*

Experiences and Activities for Preschool Children

▢ Suggest choices to children. For example, say, *You might try...* or, *Perhaps another puzzle would be more challenging*, instead of, *Do this.*

▢ Limit the number of choices offered to three. Too many choices can overwhelm young children.

▢ Engage the children in a discussion about strategies for making choices (weighing pros and cons, thinking about consequences, asking for help, and so on).

▢ Teach the children the concept of assuming responsibility for choices. Children learn this best as they are allowed to experience the consequences of their choices. For example, if Evan chooses to play Keep Away with two of his friends, he is assuming responsibility for being a contributing member of the game. If after a few minutes he decides to quit, there are consequences. Namely, his

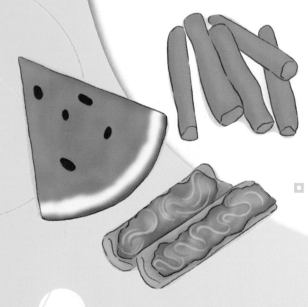

friends are left with not enough players to continue their game. Explain this consequence to Evan, and encourage him to rethink his choice. Offer suggestions: He can find a replacement to assume his spot. He can continue to play until his friends also decide to quit. He can wait until another friend expresses interest in playing. If he chooses to leave without thinking of his friends, point out that next time his friends may not allow him to join their game.

▢ Offer children choices for snacks and meals.

- Involve children in decision-making activities. Allow them a vote when choosing things like paint colors or where to hang a picture.
- Model thoughtful choice-making skills, and verbalize your decision-making process when appropriate. This will help children learn to think through options and consequences in a responsible way.
- Describe types of choices in terms of *healthy, safe, kind,* and *smart* instead of *good* or *bad. Good* or *bad* implies judgment. Using precise words like *healthy* and *kind* helps define choices.

Experiences and Activities for School-Age Children
- Discuss strategies for being a wise consumer (researching an item you wish to buy, making price comparisons).
- Increase the number of choices children make for themselves as they grow in age and maturity.
- Evaluate decisions and choices that others (characters in literature, on the news, or on television) make.

Ideas to Use with Two or More Children

- Provide multiple activities so that the children can have the experience of making their own choices. For example, offer a variety of puzzles instead of only one. Or, if you want to develop the children's eye-hand coordination, you might provide two options: scissors with magazine pictures to cut out as well as tracing paper with patterns and markers for tracing.
- Invite children to help select sites for field trips, books to read, and activities for outdoors.
- Try money-making activities such as a sidewalk art sale or a carnival. Let the children decide how to spend or donate the proceeds.

Books for Infants and Toddlers

Opposites by Sandra Boyton
Quiet Loud by Leslie Patricelle
Yummy Yucky by Leslie Patricelle

Books for Preschool Children

David Decides about Thumb Sucking by Susan M. Heitler
A Fish Out of Water by Helen Palmer
I Was So Mad by Mercer Mayer
"More, More, More," Said the Baby by Vera Williams
Peter's Chair by Ezra Jack Keats
The Three Billy Goats Gruff (any version)
The Three Little Pigs (any version)
The Little Red Hen by Byron Barton

Books for School-Age Children

The Care and Keeping of You: A Body Book for Girls by Valorie Schaefer
The Diary of a Wimpy Kid, series by Jeff Kinney
Ramona Quimby, Age 8 by Beverly Cleary

Want to Read More?

Fraser, M. W., Nash, J. K., Galinsky, M. J., & Darwin, K. E. 2000. *Making choices: Social problem-solving skills for children.* Washington, DC: NASW Press.

Jensen, E. 2008. *Brain-based learning: The new paradigm of teaching.* New York: Corwin Press.

Schwartz, B. 2005. *The paradox of choice: Why more is less.* New York: HarperCollins.

Vartanian, O. & Mandel, D. R., eds. 2011. *Neuroscience of decision making.* East Sussex, UK: Psychology Press.

I Feel Blue

COLOR AND THE BRAIN

Recent brain research confirms that color affects our mood and behavior. Shades of blue are calming and increase feelings of well-being, with sky blue being the most tranquilizing color. When you see blue, your brain releases eleven neurotransmitters that bring relaxing calmness to the body. The effects can lower body temperature and reduce perspiration and appetite. Greens are also calming. Reds and yellows are energizing (these colors also encourage creativity). Red is an engaging and emotive color, so red may tend to disturb an anxious person, while red may excite a calm person. Red triggers the pituitary and adrenal glands, enhances the sense of smell, and can increase breathing and appetite. Yellow is the color that most readily holds the brain's attention. Brown promotes a sense of security and relaxation and reduces fatigue. A textured gray is neutral. Off-white, yellow, and beige are optimal for positive feeling. Darker colors lower stress and increase feelings of peacefulness. See the chart below for more information on colors and their brain-related impact.

Most researchers agree that the impact of colors on moods and emotions is temporary because the brain ignores things that are routine. Balance the use of routine and novelty when using color for its impact.

Babies are born seeing only black and white. It takes 10 weeks of visually interacting with the environment before a newborn's brain begins to register other colors. The first color to emerge is red (around two-and-a-half months), followed by green, blue, and yellow around five months. After six months of experience viewing colors, the brain registers white as a separate color and not just the part of the black and white background from which colors have been emerging. Black will become its own separate color around 12 months. (Ramey & Ramey, 1999).

Color	Impact
red	Creates alertness and excitement Encourages creativity Increases appetite May be disturbing to anxious individual
blue	Creates a sense of well-being Sky blue is tranquilizing Can lower temperature Inhibits appetite
yellow	Creates a positive feeling Optimum color for maintaining attention Encourages creativity
orange	Increases alertness
green	Creates calmness
purple	Creates calmness
brown	Promotes a sense of security and relaxation Reduces fatigue
off-white	Creates positive feelings Helps maintain attention

BABIES ARE BORN SEEING ONLY BLACK AND WHITE.

Start Smart, Revised

Ideas for Using Color to
Enhance Learning and Influence Mood

Experiences and Activities for Infants and Toddlers

- Provide bright colors in the environment. Infants need to be exposed to colors to develop the wiring in the brain that recognizes colors.
- Use brightly colored vinyl placemats to create a crawling path on the floor.
- Place colorful mats or pieces of fabric under baby's toys.
- Display colorful mobiles or photos by the changing table.
- Use crib linens in cool colors (blue, green, purple).
- Place red placemats under the plates of children who are picky eaters. Wrap red fabric around bottles for younger children.

Experiences and Activities for Preschool Children

- Place calming colors (blues, beige tones, greens) in quiet areas or places reserved for reflection. Avoid using bright colors in these areas. (Also see pages 15–20 for ideas on how to use aromas in quiet areas.)
- Choose colors for painting depending on children's moods.
- Invite children to use colored markers and colored pencils in their drawings and writings. Ask the children how they feel about the colors they use.
- Display a yellow placemat, yellow vase of flowers, or yellow pencil holder in places where children need to be attentive.
- Wear a yellow or off-white apron or smock when presenting information.

Experiences and Activities for School-Age Children

- Teach children about the effects of colors on their moods, appetites, and behaviors. Ask questions: *Do you feel calm when you are around the color blue? Does the color red increase your appetite? Does the color yellow help you be attentive?* After the children have had experiences with the impact of color, ask them if they agree with the research about colors and their impact.
- Have children try their own color experiments. Ask the children, *Do you notice your mood or behavior changing when you are around certain colors? Try using reds to encourage appetite, blues to subdue appetite. Does it work?*

- Engage the children in a discussion about color-related phrases, such as *blue Monday, feeling blue, seeing red,* and so on. Do the phrases and their meanings match their experience?
- Display art from different artists (Mondrian, Miro, Van Gogh). Discuss the colors the artists use and how the colors create emotional reactions related to the art. Examine art from Picasso's Blue Period, for example.

Ideas to Use with Two or More Children

- Use a red marker to list the children's ideas when you challenge them to brainstorm solutions to a problem.
- Let children dictate a story about or recall the sequence of events of a field trip. Use brightly colored chalk or markers to record their dictation.
- Use reds and yellows in the dramatic play, block, and art centers. These colors increase creativity.
- Hang crepe paper streamers from sections of the ceiling to elicit specific moods in those areas. For example, dark colors in a reading area and bright colors in an art area.
- Engage the children in a discussion about colors. Find out what each child's favorite color is. See if children associate feelings with different colors.
- Think about the effect of color when planning activities such as family night. Too many bright colors may overstimulate an already excited group of children.

Books for Infants and Toddlers

Black on White by Tana Hoban
I Love Colors by Margaret Miller

Books for Preschool Children

A Color of His Own by Leo Lionni
Colors by Richard L. Allington
Is It Red? Is It Yellow? Is It Blue? by Tana Hoban
Red Is Best by Kathy Stinson

Books for School-Age Children

A Book About Colors by Mark Gonyea
My Many Colored Days by Dr. Seuss
Picasso by Mike Venezia

Want to Read More?

Jensen, E. 2008. *Brain-based learning: The new paradigm of teaching.* New York: Corwin Press.

Ramey, C. & Ramey, S. 1999. *Right from birth: Building your child's foundation for life.* New York: Goddard Press.

Schwartz, S. H. 2004. *Visual perception.* New York: McGraw-Hill.

Start Smart, Revised

Always Across

CROSS-LATERAL MOVEMENT AND THE BRAIN

CHAPTER FOUR

CROSS-LATERAL MOVEMENTS ARE MOVEMENTS THAT CROSS THE MIDLINE OF THE BODY.

Cross-lateral movements can have a dramatic effect on learning. Cross-lateral movements are movements that cross the midline of the body. Imagine a line that runs down the middle of the body, separating it in half vertically from head to toe. This is the body's midline. The left side of the brain controls the right side of the body, and the right side of the brain controls the body's left side. Cross-lateral movements encourage the two sides of the brain to communicate by stimulating the corpus callosum (line of nerves connecting the hemispheres).

Every task we approach is accomplished more efficiently and effectively when both sides of the brain are participating. Generally the brain operates utilizing both hemispheres. However, research suggests that every 90 minutes or so, beginning around six o'cock each morning, the normal hormone levels in the body peak, causing the brain to get "stuck" on the right or left side depending on which side is being used dominantly at that moment in time. The use of cross-lateral movement is an easy way to "unstick" the brain so both sides of the brain are engaged and learning is efficient and effective (Dennison & Dennison, 2010).

Ideas for Using Cross-Lateral Movements to Impact Learning

Experiences and Activities for Infants and Toddlers

☐ Babies are born with only 10 percent integration between the two hemispheres of their brains. Full integration of the brain and the resulting development of the corpus callosum continues over the first year of life, assisted by cross-lateral movements (Bartkovich & Kjos, 1988). These movements take place naturally as babies move around, learn to crawl, and even while they eat. Sucking is a cross-lateral movement. (Pretend to suck on a straw, and you will feel your tongue make a circle.) To assist the development of the brain's hemisphere integration, spend a few minutes each day crossing baby's arms across her chest or crossing her legs from one side to the other (Hanniford, 2007).

> CROSS-LATERAL MOVEMENTS TAKE PLACE NATURALLY AS BABIES MOVE AROUND, LEARN TO CRAWL, AND EVEN WHILE THEY EAT.

☐ Arrange toys to encourage babies to reach across their midlines. Arrange food on their trays to encourage them to reach for the food. Most babies do not yet have a dominant hand, so be creative in your arrangements. Give a baby something to hold with one hand, and offer an inviting toy or snack so that the baby will have to reach across with the other hand to pick it up.

☐ Create a tactile crawling pathway for toddlers. Place squares of textured fabric on the floor, and encourage children to crawl over the path. Talk with the toddlers about how the fabrics feel as they crawl.

Experiences and Activities for Preschool Children

☐ Start each day with exercises that require cross-lateral movements, such as twisting at the waist with arms stretched to the side or bending at the waist to touch toes using the left hand to touch the right toe and the right hand to touch the left toe.

- Sing songs and repeat chants using hand motions that cross the midline of the body, such as "Doodlely-Do," "Hot Cross Buns," and "Pat-a-Cake."

Doodlely-Do—Perform these movements in rhythm with this chant. The children clap their thighs twice, clap their hands twice, and then cross their hands in front of their body four times (left hand on top twice, then right hand on top twice). Then the children touch their noses, then their right shoulders with their left hands. Then the children touch their noses, then their left shoulders with their right hands. Then the children move their hands in "talking" motion just above their shoulders, then above their heads. Repeat these actions throughout the song.

Please sing to me that sweet melody
Called Doodlely-Do, Doodlely-Do.
I like the rest, but the one I like best
Goes Doodlely-Do, Doodlely-Do.
It's the simplest thing, there isn't much to it.
All you gotta do is Doodlely-Do it.
I like it so that wherever I go
It's the Doodlely, Doodlely-Do.

HAND MOTIONS THAT CROSS
THE MIDLINE OF THE BODY

Hot Cross Buns—Group the children in pairs. Have the partners stand, facing each other. As they sing the words below, the children slap their own knees, clap their own hands, touch their partner's right hand with their own right hand, slap their own knees, clap their own hands, touch their partner's left hand with their own left hand. Repeat the song once, then end by slapping their own knees, clapping their own hands, and touching both of their partner's hands with their own hands.

Hot cross buns.
Hot cross buns.
One a penny,
Two a penny,
Hot cross buns.

☐ Vary movements to traditional songs such as "Where Is Thumbkin?" and "Itsy Bitsy Spider."

Where Is Thumbkin?—When you bring each finger out from behind your back, bring them across your midline. This way, the children will learn to cross their hands in front of their bodies when they make their fingers talk to each other.

Where is Thumbkin? (Keep hands behind back.)
Where is Thumbkin?
Here I am. Here I am. (Bring out right thumb, then left.)
How are you today, sir? (Bend right thumb.)
Very well, I thank you. (Bend left thumb.)
Run away. (Put right thumb behind back.)
Run away. (Put left thumb behind back.)

Itsy Bitsy Spider
The itsy, bitsy spider went up the water spout. (Use right hand to crawl up left arm.)
Down came the rain and washed the spider out. (Swoosh hands down diagonally from left to right and then from right to left.)
Out came the sun and dried up all the rain. (Make a big circle using both arms.)
And the itsy, bitsy spider climbed up the spout again. (Use right hand to crawl up left arm.)

☐ Make up hand jives with the children. For example, slap the right hand on the left knee and then clap hands in the center of the body. Slap the left hand on the right knee and clap hands. Then snap fingers several times while crossing hand over hand, left over right and then right over left. Repeat sequence.

☐ Play songs that focus on body movements such as "Itsy Bitsy Spider," "Ram Sam Sam," and "Five Little Ducks." If crossing the midline is not part of the song, add motions that include cross-lateral movements.

☐ Teach children simple dances from the 1950s and 1960s like the Twist, the Pony, and the Stroll. Each dance includes steps that require crossing the midline. If you need directions, search the Internet or use the following sites:

http://www.jitterbuzz.com/dance50.html

(directions for the Stroll and Hand Jive)
http://www.sixtiescity.com/Culture/dance.shtm (directions
for the Twist, Pony, Madison, Watusi, Chicken and more)

- Invite the children to dance using streamers
  and scarves. Encourage the children to swing
  the streamers and scarves across their bodies.
- Play waltz music. Invite the children to remove
  their shoes and "skate" in their socks.
  Encourage the children to swing their arms from
  side to side in front of them.
- Walk on a balance beam. If a balance beam is not
  available, use a strip of masking tape on the floor.
  Encourage the children to swing their arms from side to
  side as they walk.
- Encourage the children to climb trees. Note: Supervise
  closely.
- Take a brisk walk outside. Encourage the children to swing
  their arms across their bodies as they walk.
- Encourage the children to stop occasionally throughout the
  day and give themselves a couple of hugs (by crossing their
  arms across their chests and squeezing) or pats on the
  back (tapping their left hands on their right shoulders
  and doing the same with their right hands on their
  left shoulders).
- Place materials, such as crayons, on the table so that the
  children must reach across the midline to grasp what they
  need.
  Note: Place materials in this way only as an activity to
  promote cross-lateral movements, not to encourage
  certain hand dominance. If you are not trying to
  encourage cross-lateral movements, then always place
  materials directly in front of children. It is important not
  to try to influence hand dominance. Children will figure
  this out by themselves.
- Encourage the children to paint with both hands when they
  are painting at an easel. Have the children reach across their
  midline as they paint.

ARMS ACROSS
THE CHEST IS A
CROSS-LATERAL
MOVEMENT.

◻ Play games that require the children to crawl on the floor. Let's Pretend works well by having the children imitate animals. Create a maze by having the children wind string back and forth across the room and then crawl through the maze they created. The alternating use of left and right hemispheres when crawling stimulates hemisphere integration. Most children cross the midline with their arms when crawling.

◻ Teach the children to tell and act out stories that require cross-lateral hand movements, such as acting out "Going on a Bear Hunt." The following is another example of a story that children will need to use cross-lateral movement to act out.

Mr. Wiggle and Mr. Waggle

This is Mr. Wiggle (hold up right fist with the thumb pointing up—wiggle thumb), *and this is Mr. Waggle* (hold up left fist with thumb pointing up—wiggle thumb). *Mr. Wiggle and Mr. Waggle live in houses on top of different hills and three hills apart.* (Put thumbs inside of fists.)

One day, Mr. Wiggle decided to visit Mr. Waggle. He opened his door (open fist), *pop, came outside* (raise thumb), *pop, and closed his door* (close fist), *pop. Then he went down the hill and up the hill, down the hill and up the hill, and down the hill and up the hill* (move right thumb down and up in a wave fashion to go with text).

When he reached Mr. Waggle's house, he knocked on the door, knock, knock, knock (use right thumb to tap left fist). *No one answered. So, Mr. Wiggle went down the hill and up the hill, down the hill and up the hill, and down the hill and up the hill to his house* (use wave motion to follow text). *When he reached his house, he opened* the door (open fist), *pop, went inside* (place thumb in palm), *pop, and closed the door* (close fist), *pop.*

The next day Mr. Waggle decided to visit Mr. Wiggle. He opened his door (open left fist), *pop, came outside* (raise thumb), *pop, and closed his door* (close fist), *pop. Then he went down the hill and up the hill, down the hill and up the hill, and down the hill and up the hill* (move thumb down and up in a wave fashion to go with text).

When he reached Mr. Wiggle's house, he knocked on the door, knock, knock, knock (use left thumb to tap right fist). *No one answered. So, Mr. Waggle went down the hill and up the hill, down the hill and up the hill, and down the hill and up the hill to his house* (use wave motion to follow text). *When he reached his house, he opened the door* (open fist), *pop, went inside* (place thumb in palm), *pop, and closed the door* (close fist), *pop.*

The next day Mr. Wiggle (shake right fist) *decided to visit Mr. Waggle, and Mr. Waggle* (shake left fist) *decided to visit Mr. Wiggle at the same time. So, they opened their doors* (open both fists), *pop, went outside* (raise thumbs), *and closed their doors* (close fists), *pop, and went down the hill and up the hill, down the hill and up the hill* (wave motion to follow text), *and they met on top of the hill.*

They talked and laughed (wiggle thumbs) *and visited until the sun went down. Then they went down the hill and up the hill, down the hill and up the hill, to their own homes* (wave motion with both hands to text). *They opened their doors* (open fists), *pop, went inside* (tuck thumbs inside), *pop, and closed the doors* (close fists), *pop, and went to sleep.* (Place your head on your hands.)

☐ Invite the children to help with simple housekeeping chores. Jobs like washing windows and setting the table require cross-lateral movement.
☐ Encourage the children to sit on your lap and read the comics section of the newspaper with you. Let the children turn the pages of the paper, a cross-lateral movement.
☐ Encourage the children to use a punching bag. Create a punching bag by stuffing a pillowcase with old nylons or rags, tying it shut, and hanging it from the ceiling.

Experiences and Activities for School-Age Children

◻ Demonstrate hemisphere control and integration. Have each child sit in a chair. Instruct the children to lift their right feet off the floor and make clockwise circles. Then, while they are making clockwise circles with their right feet, try to draw the number six in the air with their right hands. What happens? This activity demonstrates a conflict in hemisphere control. The left hemisphere is controlling the movements on the right side of the body (foot circling), but when the children try to draw the numeral six, which requires moving counter-clockwise, it is difficult for that same hemisphere to control a movement that goes in the opposite direction. Now try this: Make clockwise circles in the air with your right foot and draw a numeral six in the air with your left hand. What do you notice?

◻ Encourage the children to make up new hand motions to "Doodlely-Do" (page 33) or to create cross-lateral movements for "Tooty Ta" (page 68) .

Ideas to Use with Two or More Children

◻ Make friendship circles. Provide a large sheet of butcher paper and crayons, and invite the children to make large interlocking circles with a friend.

◻ Play the traditional outdoor games of Keep Away, Wall Ball, and Horseshoes with variations that allow them to include cross-lateral movement.

Keep Away—Divide the children into two teams. One team starts tossing the ball back and forth between team members, attempting to keep the ball away from members of the other team. When the second team manages to get control of the ball, the children in that group attempt to keep the ball away from the first team. The ball must stay in motion at all times.

Wall Ball—Provide the children with a tennis ball. Have the children toss the ball against the wall. After throwing the ball, challenge the children to cross their midlines with their arms before catching the ball as it bounces back. Change the activities by asking the children to cross their midline with each leg before they catch the ball.

Horseshoes—Arrange the game so that the children must toss the rubber horseshoes across their midlines in order to get the horseshoes on the stake. For example, have the children stand perpendicular to the stake before tossing their horseshoes.

☐ Teach the children simple square-dance steps. The do-si-do and promenade provide great cross-lateral movements. Encourage the children to make up new dances using these and other square-dance steps. Resources include http://www.folkdancecamp.org/Dances.html and http://www.ehow.com/how_2049302_learn-square-dance.html. Encourage the children to create puppet shows. Moving puppets across the stage will require crossing the midline.

☐ Teach the children how to shake hands and to double shake (left hand to friend's left hand and right hand to friend's right hand). Stop several times a day to shake hands with a friend.

Books for Infants and Toddlers

Baby Danced the Polka by Karen Beaumont
Head, Shoulders, Knees, and Toes and Other Rhymes by Zita Newcome

Books for Preschool Children

Clap Your Hands by Lorinda Bryan Cauley
Dance, Tanya by Patricia Lee Gauch
Every Time I Climb a Tree by David McCord
Hand Rhymes by Marc Brown
Skates by Ezra Jack Keats
Song and Dance Man by Karen Ackerman

Books for School-Age Children

The Complete Book of Figure Skating by Carole Shulman

Ivy and Bean Doomed to Dance by Sophie Blackall

Schoolyard Rhymes: Kids' Own Rhymes for Rope Skipping, Hand Clapping, Ball Bouncing, and Just Plain Fun by Judy Sierra and Melissa Sweet

Want to Read More?

Barkovich, A. J. & Kjos, B. O. 1988. Normal postnatal development of the corpus callosum as demonstrated by MR imaging. *American Journal of Neuroradiology.* 9, 487–491.

Dennison, P. & Dennison, G. 2010. *Brain gym: Teacher's edition,* revised. Ventura, CA: Edu-kinesthetics.

Hannaford, C. 2005. *Smart moves: Why learning is not all in your head,* revised. Salt Lake City, UT: Great Rivers Publications.

I Feel, I Remember

EMOTIONS AND THE BRAIN

Emotions play an important role in our reactions, memory, and motivation. In the center of the brain is the amygdala, which is the seat of emotion. When incoming information enters the brain, it is the amygdala that reacts. The amygdala protects us from harm by triggering the "fight or flight" hormone (adrenaline) when we encounter a threat or danger.

The amygdala also plays a role in memory and learning. When information enters the brain, it is routed through the amygadala where it is provided a "code" for processing. When the information has emotional content or when it is of high interest to the learner, that information receives a high priority for processing. Not only will this high-priority coding increase the chance that the information will make it to long-term memory, it will also make the learning indelible (Sousa, 2005). It is, then, easy to see why we remember most easily life's highs and lows. Researchers believe that this is because emotions act as a memory fixative. If you recall your most vivid memories, you will notice that the memories that come to mind first are the ones that are accompanied by strong emotions.

Consider the following connections between emotions and the brain:

- Several studies have demonstrated a link between emotion and motivation. Strong negative emotions inhibit our ability to think. For example, an argument at breakfast can distract us for the rest of the day. Learning is enhanced by positive feelings and inhibited by negative feelings (Jensen, 2008).

- Top brain scientists say that emotions are a key part of the logic and reasoning processes. The brain makes better decisions when some emotion is present (Jensen, 2008).

- Emotions are contagious (Goleman, 2006). When we are near someone who is cheerful and upbeat, we feel better, too.

- Positive emotions do more than reflect contentment. They help babies learn. Babies who feel good are more alert, attentive, and responsive, and they remember better, too (Ramey & Ramey, 1999).

- Toddlers develop a sense of self when they are around 15- to 18-months old. At that age, their range of emotions expands to include new self-conscious ones (pride, embarrassment, shame). These complex emotions intensify the links between thinking and feeling and can be influenced by a caregiver's behavior (Ramey & Ramey, 1999).

* Additional research on page 168 in the Appendix.

Ideas for Using Emotions to Enhance Learning and Mood

Experiences and Activities for Infants and Toddlers

- Be joyful when playing with infants and toddlers. Joy is contagious.
- Set the tone with a smile. Babies are particularly sensitive to facial expressions.
- Sing to infants on a regular basis. Singing most often evokes emotion.
- Describe and label the emotions that you notice babies displaying.

Experiences and Activities for Preschool Children

- Smile. Be upbeat. A positive mood can affect the mood of the group.
- Engage the children in a discussion about feelings and how they affect us. Describe how

POSITIVE EMOTIONS DO MORE THAN REFLECT CONTENTMENT. THEY HELP CHILDREN LEARN.

feelings can help us work out sadness, share joy, express discontent, resolve problems and conflicts, calm our spirits, and balance our lives. Part of helping children attach emotion to learning is helping them understand and express emotions.

■ Sing throughout the day. Songs generally fill us with positive emotions. Try some of the songs below. A book with a great comprehensive collection of songs is *Rise Up Singing* edited by Peter Blood and Annie Patterson. If you cannot sing, then just hum a tune, or chant the words to songs.

If You're Happy and You Know It

(Act out the motions indicated in the song.)

If you're happy and you know it, clap your hands.
If you're happy and you know it, clap your hands.
If you're happy and you know it,
Then your face will surely show it.
If you're happy and you know it, clap your hands.

Create as many verses as you like. Suggestions for additional verses:
Stomp your feet!
Pat your head!
Say hello!

The More We Get Together

The more we get together, together, together,
The more we get together, the happier we'll be!
For your friends are my friends and my friends are your friends.
The more we get together, the happier we'll be!

Twinkle, Twinkle, Little Star

Twinkle, twinkle, little star,
How I wonder what you are!
Up above the world so high,
Like a diamond in the sky.
Twinkle, twinkle, little star,
How I wonder what you are.

Boom, Boom, Ain't It Great to Be Crazy?

A horse and a flea and three blind mice,
Sat on a curbstone shooting dice,
The horse he slipped and fell on the flea,
"Whoops!" said the flea "There's a horse on me!"

Chorus:

Boom, boom, ain't it great to be crazy?
Boom, boom, ain't it great to be crazy?
Giddy and foolish the whole day through,
Boom, boom, ain't it great to be crazy?

Way down South where bananas grow,
A flea stepped on an elephant's toe.
The elephant cried with tears in
his eyes,
"Why don't you pick on
someone your size?"
(Chorus)

Way up North where there's
ice and show,
There lived a penguin, and his
name was Joe.
He got so tired of black and white,
He wore pink slacks to the dance last night.
(Chorus)

☐ Help children see the need for what they
are learning. Connect the joy of being self-sufficient and the joy of feeling
accomplished to the things children are able to do when they can read. For
example, the ability to read allows you to enjoy a storybook, follow rules for
a game, know what your friend is saying in a letter, and determine which
candy bar has your favorite ingredients. Math helps you know how
many more days until your birthday, how much money you need
to buy a new ball, and so on.

EMOTIONS ARE
CONTAGIOUS!

- Add surprises. Invite a funny or interesting character to "pop in" to deliver some important information (see pages 65–70).
- Use stories with emotional messages to help children learn concepts.

Story	Concept
Itsy Bitsy Spider	Try, try again
The Tenth Good Thing About Barney	Death
Amazing Grace	Believing in yourself
A Chair for My Mother	Cooperation, respect, love
Alexander and the Terrible, Horrible, No Good, Very Bad Day	Everyone has a bad day once in a while
Owl Moon	Father/child relationship, nature
Love You Forever	Security
Owl Babies	Fear
Feelings	Feelings
Don't Be Afraid, Little Pip	Fear
Mama Zooms	Joy with Mom
Going Home	Celebration

- Teach relaxation strategies such as deep breathing, thinking of a peaceful place, and exercising. Relieving stress helps us tap into positive emotions.
- Express your emotions openly. Let the children see you happy, sad, angry, peaceful, and content.
- Discuss the emotional events of your life, such as your high school graduation, a recent wedding, or a family picnic. If there are photographs of these events, show them to the children.
- When talking about their memories of events, ask the children if they can remember how they felt at the time. Ask the children how the memory makes them feel now.

> IN THE CENTER OF THE BRAIN IS THE AMYGDALA, WHICH IS THE SEAT OF EMOTION.

☐ Discuss the emotions involved in celebrations. Count and describe the many emotions in celebrating a birthday, a holiday, a wedding, or the birth of a sibling.

Experiences and Activities for School-Age Children

☐ Engage the children in a discussion about emotions. Explain that emotions are expressions of our feelings and that understanding emotions and managing them help us develop self-control and create balance in our lives. Being able to attach emotion to learning is contingent upon children understanding the role emotions play in their lives.

☐ Explain that emotions are contagious. Have the children experiment with smiling. Can they cause another child to smile?

☐ Explore jokes and humor by occasionally telling child-sized jokes, reading funny stories, singing funny songs, and playing nonsense games. Embrace the children's often imperfect attempts at humor.

☐ Discuss how characters in storybooks display, use, and control their emotions.

☐ Connect applications to learning. Point out the joy associated with being able to solve problems and do things on our own. For example, fractions help us divide things fairly. This makes everyone happy. Using concrete examples will help children see the connection between the skill and its use. Have children divide a sandwich or a candy bar into four equal parts.

Ideas to Use with
Two or More Children

☐ Use drama. Children love playing with puppets, role playing, and acting out stories or plays. The children's emotional interaction with a play or story will help them remember and learn the message of the story.

☐ Let the children know you care about them. Notice when they are absent. Celebrate their return to class. Ask about their experiences. Celebrate their successes. Share their dismay at repeated failure. Encourage persistence.

Books for Infants and Toddlers

Baby Dance by Ann Taylor
Baby Faces by Margaret Miller

Books for Preschool Children

Alexander and the Terrible, Horrible, No Good, Very Bad Day by Judith Viorst
Amazing Grace by Mary Hoffman
A Chair for My Mother by Vera B. Williams
Feelings by Joanne Murphy
Frog Is Frightened by Max Velthuijs
Going Home by Eve Bunting
The Kissing Hand by Audrey Penn
Love You Forever by Robert Munch
Mama Zooms by Jane Cowen-Fletcher
Owl Babies by Martin Waddell
Owl Moon by Jane Yolen

> STRONG NEGATIVE EMOTIONS INHIBIT OUR ABILITY TO THINK.

Books for School-Age Children

Diary of a Wimpy Kid by Jeff Kinney
Ramona the Pest by Beverly Cleary

Want to Read More?

Cozolino, L. 2006. *The neuroscience of human relationships.* New York: Norton.

Gilkey, R., Caceda, R., & Kilts, C. 2010. When emotional reasoning trumps IQ. *Harvard Business Review* 88: 27.

Goleman, D. 1998. *Working with emotional intelligence.* New York: Bantam.

Goleman, D. 2005. *Social intelligence: The new science of human relationships.* New York: Bantam

Jensen, E. 2008. *Brain-based learning: The new paradigm of teaching.* New York: Corwin Press.

Ramey, C. & Ramey, S. 1999. *Right from birth: Building your child's foundation for life.* New York: Goddard Press.

Salovey, P., Brackett, M. A., & Mayer, J., eds. 2004. *Emotional intelligence: Key readings in the Mayer and Salovey model.* Port Chester, NY: Dude Press.

Sousa, D. 2005. *How the brain learns.* New York: Corwin Press.

Hop, Skip, Jump

EXERCISE AND THE BRAIN

Exercise is beneficial to both the body and the brain. Regular workouts on the playground or in the gym improve attention span, memory, and learning. Regular exercise also reduces stress and the effects of attention-deficit hyperactivity disorder (ADHD), and can even delay cognitive decline as we age (Ratey & Hagerman, 2008).

Exercise pumps more blood throughout the body, including to the brain. More blood means more oxygen and, therefore, better-nourished brain tissue.

The increase in oxygen flow also supports the function of neurotransmitters as they send impulses from neuron to neuron across synaptic gaps (Sousa, 2005).

Exercise causes the brain to produce more of a protein called brain-derived neurotrophic factor. This powerful protein encourages brain cells to grow, interconnect, and communicate in new ways.

Exercise almost instantly increases the presence of dopamine and norepinephrine and keeps them elevated for a period of time so that the effect is like a small dose of Ritalin or Adderall, medicines used by children who are diagnosed with ADHD. Exercise also helps to reduce impulsivity and the desire for immediate gratification as it works to wake up the executive function of the frontal cortex, which helps us delay gratification, make better choices, and add time to evaluate the consequences of an action (Ratey & Hagerman, 2008).

Consider the following connections between exercise and the brain:

- People who exercise regularly have improved short-term memory and exhibit faster reaction time. Exercisers also demonstrate higher levels of creativity than nonexercisers (Steinberg et al., 1997).
- Physical exercise stimulates a quick rise and fall of adrenaline that parallels the rise and fall of adrenaline that occurs when we face challenges or problems (see pages 119–127).
- Ratey and Hagerman (2008) say that exercise may also be the best way to increase neurogenesis, which is the daily process by which the brain makes new neurons.
- When children exercise they are building muscle and they are boosting their brainpower. Exercise increases key proteins that help build the brain's infrastructure for learning and memory (van Praag, 2009).

* Additional research on page 169 in the Appendix.

Ideas for Using Exercise to Build Brain Power

Experiences and Activities for Infants and Toddlers

- Exercise babies' arms and legs during tummy time or after changing a baby's diaper.
- Teach toddlers simple exercises like toe touches.
- Provide space for infants and toddlers to move. Refrain from using walkers, swings, carriers, and any equipment that inhibits movement. The fertile time for wiring the foundation of physical skills is between birth and two years.
  - Encourage little ones to chase bubbles.
  - Play movement games. Here are few suggestions:

Musical Freeze—Invite your walkers to dance or move in a circle while a favorite song plays. Occasionally stop the music. When

REGULAR EXERCISE IMPROVES ATTENTION SPAN, MEMORY, AND LEARNING.

you stop the music, the children also stop moving. When you start the music again, the children begin to move again.

Cat and Mouse—This is a simple game of chase. Pretend to be a cat and chase a child who pretends to be a mouse.

Animal Antics—Demonstrate an animal movement (stretch like a cat, fly like a bird, swim like a fish) and invite the children to copy your movements or make up their own movements.

Experiences and Activities for Preschool Children

- ☐ Use music and movement activities every day.
- ☐ Have the children exercise to music or exercise CDs. Music adds to the fun and helps keep the rhythm moving and the pace upbeat.
- ☐ Teach children simple dances. Children love to do the Chicken Dance and the Bunny Hop.
- ☐ Teach the children about health and fitness. Focus on the positive effects of exercise on both mental and physical abilities.
- ☐ Provide a stethoscope and invite children to listen to their hearts beat. Encourage each child to do 25 jumping jacks and then use the stethoscope to listen to his or her heartbeat a second time. What's different?
- ☐ Make exercise bands from 3' lengths of 1"-wide elastic. Provide each child with an exercise band. Have the children stand on part of the band and use their hands to stretch their bands over their heads. The children then hold the bands in front of them and stretch the bands across their chests. Next, the children place the bands over their heads and behind their necks. Finally, have the children stretch their hands forward. Encourage the children to create their own stretches.
- ☐ Create an exercise program. Schedule an exercise time each day or at least several times a week.
- ☐ Model exercises for the children, such as running laps on a playground, taking hikes, or riding a bike.
- ☐ Provide equipment that encourages active play outdoors. This includes balls, jump ropes, and plastic hoops.

Experiences and Activities for School-Age Children

- Play Left Shoulder, Right Shoulder. Gently toss a soft ball to a child, and call out, "Left shoulder." The child then tries to hit the ball with her left shoulder. Toss the ball again, and call out, "Right foot," "Right elbow," "Left knee," and so on.
- Take a field trip to a local gym, YMCA, or YWCA. Talk with the children about how the people are exercising—running, swimming, playing basketball, playing soccer, doing yoga, taking gymnastics, and so on.
- Encourage the children to create exercise routines and then teach their routines to friends.

Ideas to Use with Two or More Children

- Play parachute games with a group. Here are few simple ones:

Ocean Waves—Children hold the edges of the parachute and raise and lower it to create waves.

Round and Round—Players try to "pass" the parachute around in one direction without crossing their hands.

Exchange Game—Players hold the parachute tightly as they sit on the ground. The players on one side lean backward to make the players on the other side rise.

Change-O—Children raise the parachute over their heads. Some children run underneath the parachute, changing places, while the remaining players hold the parachute up and gradually let it drift to the ground.

Poppers—Place several small balls (tennis balls, Ping Pong balls) on a parachute. The players bounce the balls on the parachute by quickly raising and lowering the parachute.

Start Smart, Revised

The following are a few more complex parachute games for older children:

Fruit Basket Turn Over—Assign each player the name of a fruit *(banana, apple, orange)*. Select one child to be the leader. When the leader calls the name of a fruit, everyone with this fruit name swaps places by running under the parachute. When the leader calls, "Fruit basket turn over," all the players place the parachute on the floor and then find a new place.

Roll Around—Place a ball on the edge of the parachute. The players attempt to get the ball to roll around the edge of the parachute in continuous motion without letting the ball fall off the parachute or roll into the center of the parachute.

◻ Teach older children rhymes to chant as they jump rope. Here are a couple of popular rhymes the children can use when there are two people turning the rope.

Benjamin Franklin went to France
To teach the ladies how to dance.
First the heel and then the toe;
Spin around, and out you go. (Jumper runs out.)

Skipping to town to see a clown.
Over hedges, under bridges,
Calling (friend's name) *to skip along.*
Together we'll sing a counting song.
One, two (Count skips until someone misses.)

(child's name) *and* (child's name), *come right in.*
(child's name) *and* (child's name), *can you spin?*
(child's name) *and* (child's name), *turn around.*
(child's name) *and* (child's name), *make a sound.*
(child's name) *and* (child's name), *wave to a friend.*
Okay, jumpers, that's the end!

Mabel, Mabel, set the table.
Do it fast as you are able.
Don't forget the salt, pepper, vinegar, mustard.
(Keep repeating the last line until the jumper misses.)

PEOPLE WHO EXERCISE REGULARLY HAVE IMPROVED SHORT-TERM MEMORY AND FASTER REACTION TIME.

Books for Infants and Toddlers

Baby Dance by Ann Taylor

From Head to Toe by Eric Carle

The Baby Dance by Kathy Henderson

Books for Preschool Children

Busy Fingers by C.W. Bowie

Clap Your Hands by Lorinda B. Cauley

Dance by Bill T. Jones

Run, Jump, Whiz, Splash by Vera Rosenberry

Shake It to the One That You Love the Best by Cheryl Warren Mattox

To Be a Kid by Maya Aimera

Books for School-Age Children

Anna Banana: 101 Jump Rope Rhymes by Joanna Cole

Amelia Bedelia Goes Camping by Peggy Parish

Want to Read More?

Hannaford, C. 2005. *Smart moves: Why learning is not all in your head,* revised. Salt Lake City, UT: Great Rivers Publications.

Ratey, J. & Hagerman, E., 2008. *Spark: The revolutionary new science of exercise and the brain.* New York: Little, Brown and Company.

Sousa, D. 2005. *How the brain learns.* New York: Corwin Press.

Steinberg, H., Sykes, E., Moss, T., Lowery, S., LeBoutillier, N., & Dewey, A. 1997. Exercise increases creativity independent of mood. *British Journal of Sports Medicine* ; 31: 240–245.

van Praag, H. 2009. Exercise and the brain: Something to chew on. *Trends in Neuroscience* 32 (5): 283–290.

Right and Left

HEMISPHERES

AND THE BRAIN

The brain is divided into two hemispheres by a thick line of nerve cells called the corpus callosum. The brain has a left hemisphere and a right hemisphere. Each hemisphere has unique functions. The corpus callosum transmits information from one side of the brain to the other. Hemisphere functions are not readily interchangeable. The tendency for each hemisphere to specialize in certain functions is referred to as *lateralization.*

The right hemisphere controls the left side of the body, and the left hemisphere controls the right side of the body. Sensory information, in general, also crosses over the hemispheres of the brain. Damage to one side of the body will affect the opposite side of the body. The chart below defines the functions specific to each hemisphere.

Left Hemisphere	Right Hemisphere
Logical and analytical thinking	Intuitive and holistic thinking
Deals with information convergently	Deals with information divergently
Processes information linearly and sequentially	Processes information diffusely and simultaneously
Makes sense of time	Makes sense of space
Responsible for verbal expression and language	Responsible for gestures, facial expressions, and body language
Responsible for determining cause and effect relationships and arithmetic operations	Responsible for relational mathematical operations
The seat of reason	The seat of passions and dreams
Recognizes words and numbers	Recognizes places, faces, and music
Controls the right side of the body	Controls the left side of the body

Current research indicates that most people have a dominant hemisphere, and that dominance affects many aspects of life. Researchers use the term *preference* as opposed to *dominance.* People whose brains prefer using left-hemisphere skills are generally verbal, analytical, and good at problem solving. People whose brains prefer to use the right hemisphere generally like to paint and draw, are good at math, and deal more easily with visual rather than verbal information (Sousa, 2008). The learning process engages both hemispheres of the brain. It is important that children's learning experiences always provide aspects that support both hemispheres.

Handedness (being right- or left-handed) and hemisphere dominance appear to have minimal connection. There is also no support for connecting brain-hemisphere preference with IQ (Toga & Thompson, 2003).

Ideas to Use Hemisphere Specializations to Enhance Learning

Experiences and Activities for Infants and Toddlers

The line of nerve cells that allows the crossover of information is not fully developed in infants and toddlers. Caregivers should focus on cross-lateral movements (see activities on pages 31–40) for this age group.

Experiences and Activities for Preschool Children

☐ Provide both visual and verbal clues when presenting information to children.
  ▪ When reading to children, stop periodically and discuss the story's events and illustrations with the children.
  ▪ Use concrete examples when teaching.
  ▪ Use story maps to help children understand stories. Story maps divide the narrative into logical, smaller units and, at the same time, illustrate the story as a whole. Story maps and graphic organizers appeal to both hemispheres.

THE BRAIN IS DIVIDED INTO TWO HEMISPHERES BY A THICK LINE OF NERVE CELLS CALLED THE CORPUS CALLOSUM.

- When discussing concepts with the children, do so both logically and intuitively.
  - Use imagery and comparison when describing a concept. Point out how a new concept is similar to another concept that is familiar to the children.
  - Ask questions that require children to think about how they feel about a concept. For example, if you are discussing zoo animals, you might ask the children what they think it feels like to live in the zoo.
  - Ask the children "what if" questions. For example, *What if zoo animals lived in our backyards instead of zoos?*
- Avoid giving the children conflicting messages. Make sure your tone, facial expressions, and body language match your words. For example, if you are talking about an upcoming trip to the zoo that will be lots of fun, make sure you have a smile on your face.
- Design activities and assessments that allow children to use both hemispheres of their brains to show what they can do and what they know.
  - Encourage children to draw pictures of their favorite parts of a story.
  - Invite children to re-enact a story.
  - Challenge children to write descriptions of how a story makes them feel. Have the children describe the emotions of the characters in a story.

THE LEARNING PROCESS ENGAGES BOTH HEMISPHERES OF THE BRAIN.

Books for Infants and Toddlers

Baby Faces by Margaret Miller
Twinkle, Twinkle, Little Star by Iza Trapani

Books for Preschool Children

Miss Mary Mack by Mary Ann Hoberman
Ten Black Dots by Donald Crews

Books for School-Age Children

My Dog's Brain by Stephen Huneck

The True Story of the Three Little Pigs by Jon Scieszka

Want to Read More?

Sousa, D. 2005. *How the brain learns.* New York: Corwin Press.

Toga, A.W., Thompson, P. M., & Sowell, E. R. 2006. Mapping brain maturation. *Trends in Neuroscience.* 29(3):148–59.

Toga A.W. & Thompson P. M. 2003. Mapping brain asymmetry. *National Review of Neuroscience.* 4(1): 37–48.

THE RIGHT HEMISPHERE CONTROLS THE LEFT SIDE OF THE BODY, AND...

THE LEFT HEMISPHERE CONTROLS THE RIGHT SIDE OF THE BODY.

Water, Water Everywhere

HYDRATION AND THE BRAIN

Not drinking enough water has detrimental effects on the brain. Without proper hydration, brain cells and other neurons shrink, and biochemical processes involved in cellular communication slow down. A drop of as little as 1–2 percent of fluid levels can result in slower brain processing speeds, cause deficits in attention, and impair short-term memory and visual tracking (Lieberman, 2007).

Children who do not get enough water may appear bored, listless, and drowsy. The amount of water a child needs to remain alert and healthy each day will vary depending on the child's age, weight, and activity level. Children need water all throughout the day. Always have water available. Encourage children to drink water whenever they wish, and always with meals and snacks.

Limit the consumption of fruit juices and sodas. Fruit juices trigger the digestive process, which drains water from cells surrounding the stomach. Living in a hot climate or exercising vigorously also increases the need for more water.

> NOT DRINKING ENOUGH WATER HAS DETRIMENTAL EFFECTS ON THE BRAIN.

> CHILDREN WHO DO NOT GET ENOUGH WATER MAY APPEAR BORED, LISTLESS, AND DROWSY.

WARNING!

Pediatricians recommend not giving water to infants under six months due to their limited kidney function and the possibility of high levels of minerals in water.

Ideas for Using Water to Enhance Brain Functions

Experiences and Activities for Infants and Toddlers

☐ Drink water throughout the day to model the importance of drinking water.

☐ Offer water in place of juice to older babies (six months and up) and to toddlers.

☐ Serve water in special cups. Consider allowing toddlers to decorate special water cups.

☐ Encourage little ones to drink water by using crazy straws for drinking water.

Experiences and Activities for Preschool Children

☐ Talk with the children about why it is important to drink water. Explain in simple terms how water helps the brain work better. Point out that brain tissue is 75–80 percent water. When we lose water through perspiration, the process of digestion, and elimination of waste, that water must be replaced. Thirsty brains have a hard time thinking.

☐ Take scheduled water breaks.

☐ Let the children have water when they ask for it. At first, they will need to go to the bathroom more frequently, but eventually their bladders will adjust. Keep water available all day long. Serve water with meals and snacks.

WATER IS A SOLVENT FOR THE CHEMICALS AND NUTRIENTS THE BODY AND BRAIN NEED.

- Provide small cups and encourage the children to decorate their cups in their own unique fashion. Keep the cups accessible for drinking water.
- Provide a small paper cup filled with water to each child. Ask them to take small sips, counting how many it takes to drink half the water. Refill the cups. Then ask them to count how many sips it takes to drink all of the water. If children aren't counting yet, have them use tally marks to record their sips.
- Make colored ice cubes by adding a little fruit juice (cherry and grape juices work great) to water in small ice cube trays and freezing the ice cubes. Provide tongs. Invite the children to sort the cubes by color, and then use them in drinks or let the ice cubes melt and then drink the melted ice.
- Provide ice cubes in zipper-closure bags. Give the children wooden blocks to use to make crushed ice, and then eat the crushed ice from their bags. This is also a good way to begin to learn about the effect of force.
- Provide ice in zipper-closure bags. Suggest that the children place the bags of ice on different items—a book, a mitten, a crayon, or a mirror—so the ice can make the items cold. Do some items get colder than others? When the children finish with the experiment and the ice melts, let the children pour the water through a funnel into individual cups and drink the melted ice.
- Invite children to place ice cubes in two zipper-closure bags. Have the children place one bag in a sunny window and the other bag in a cool place. Which one melts first? After the ice melts, pour the water into individual cups and let the children drink it.
- Have the children wash their hands and then sculpt shaved ice into their own creations. When the children finish making their creations, encourage them to eat their sculptures.
- Encourage the children to drink water after they brush their teeth or when they take a bathroom break. This creates opportunities to add drinking water to existing routines.

ENCOURAGE CHILDREN TO DRINK WATER.

- Demonstrate the effect of water on plants. Provide two plants. Water one on a regular basis, and do not water the second one at all. After a week or so, or maybe sooner, the effect on the plant that did not receive water should be visible.

Experiences and Activities for School-Age Children

- Explain how the brain uses water. Point out that brain tissue is 75–80 percent water. When we lose water through perspiration, the process of digestion, and elimination of waste, we must replace it. Water helps dilute body chemicals and transport elements and glucose. Here are the ways that water supports brain functions.
  - Water is a solvent for the chemicals and nutrients the body and brain need. For example, the carbohydrates and proteins that the body uses as food are metabolized and then transported by water in the bloodstream. (Equally important is the ability of water to transport waste material out of our bodies.)
  - Water is key to many chemical reactions. For example, water breaks down the chemicals that transmit nerve impulses across the synapses in the brain once those chemicals have done their jobs.
  - Blood brings oxygen (for alertness) and glucose (for energy) to the brain. Blood is 80 percent water. Water's "stickiness" (from surface tension) plays a part in our body's ability to transport these materials.
  - Water helps to keep the body cool because it takes a lot of heat energy to increase water temperature by even a small amount.
- Demonstrate surface tension with one or both of following experiments:
  - Give each child an eyedropper, a piece of wax paper, a cup of plain water, and a cup of soapy water. Ask the children to use the eyedroppers to drop water onto a sheet of wax paper and to observe the drops. Then have the children use the eyedroppers to drop soapy water onto the wax paper and to observe the drops. *What differences do you observe between the two different drops?*
    - Use an eyedropper to drop water onto a penny. Use a second eyedropper to drop soapy water on a second penny. *Which penny holds the most water? Why?*

Background information: The surface tension of water is caused by the attraction of water molecules to each other, just as a magnet is attracted to metal. Soap reduces the surface tension of water by disrupting the hydrogen bonds between the water molecules.

Ideas to Use with Two or More Children

- Invite a small group of children to have a contest with a friend to see who can hold a mouthful of water for the longest amount of time before swallowing it.
- Encourage the children to drink water from a long straw and a short straw. Have a contest in which one child drinks four ounces of water with a long straw and another child drinks the same amount of water with a short straw. What happens? (Make a very long straw by taping several straws together.)
- Provide crazy straws and cups of water for each child. Which child can empty a glass of water first using a crazy straw?

Books for Infants and Toddlers

Drinking Water by Mari Schuh
Splash! by Roberta Grobel Intrater

Books for Preschool Children

Water by J. M. Parramon
Water Is Wet by Penny Pollock
The Water's Journey by Eleonore Schmid

Books for School-Age Children

A Cool Drink of Water by Barbara Kerley
A Drop of Water by Walter Wick
My Water Comes from the Mountains by Tiffany Fourment

BRAIN TISSUE
IS 75–80 PERCENT
WATER.

Want to Read More?

Batmanghelidj, F. 2008. *Your body's many cries for water*, third edition. Los Angeles, CA: Global Health Solutions, Inc.

Lieberman, H. R. 2007. Hydration and cognition: A critical review and recommendations for future research. *Journal of the American College of Nutrition*. 26: 555S–561S.

Laughter and Learning

LAUGHTER AND THE BRAIN

Laughter increases white blood cell activity and changes the chemical balance of the blood (Jensen, 2008). Researchers believe laughter boosts the body's production of chemicals such as serotonin, which are needed for alertness and memory. Laughter reduces stress, and low stress enhances the brain's receptivity to learning. According to researchers, laughter and having fun can also boost the body's immune system (through the production of interleukins) for as long as three days—the day of the fun and the next two.

Studies show that humor may give people a natural high by activating the same reward centers in the brain that have previously been linked with happiness and drug-induced euphoria.

> LAUGHTER INCREASES WHITE BLOOD CELL ACTIVITY AND CHANGES THE CHEMICAL BALANCE OF THE BLOOD (JENSEN, 2008).

Laughter and the chemicals it releases in the body can improve symptoms of depression, primarily by reducing stress. In other words, laughter can help counteract the negative health consequences of chronic stress. By laughing, you can boost both your mind and your body.

Ideas for Using Laughter to Boost Memory and the Immune System

Experiences and Activities for Infants and Toddlers

- Wear a silly hat or big sunglasses while changing diapers or playing with little ones.
- Play tickle games like those described below:

'Round the House
'Round the house, 'round the house, (Use your finger to lightly draw a circle on baby's palm.)
Goes the little mousie.
Up the stairs, up the stairs, (Walk your index finger and middle finger up the baby's arm.)
In the little housie. (Lightly tickle the baby under the arm.)

Washington Square
From here to there to Washington Square (Hold baby's hand palm up and use your index finger to draw a light square)
When I get there, I'll tickle your hair. (Tickle baby's hair.)

- Play chasing games with toddlers.
- Play Peekaboo. Hide your face behind your hands at the beginning of the game. Gradually change to use other items to hide your face (a blanket, a piece of paper, a book).

LAUGHTER REDUCES STRESS, AND LOW STRESS ENHANCES THE BRAIN'S RECEPTIVITY TO LEARNING.

Experiences and Activities for Preschool Children

☐ Sing silly songs (see pages 81–87). Here are three songs children find humorous:

Down by the Bay

Down by the bay
Where the watermelons grow.
Back to my home
I dare not go.
For if I do
My mother will say,
"Did you ever see a bear
combing his hair?"
Down by the bay.

Sing the song again, changing the second-to-last line to refer to a bee with a sunburned knee, moose kissing a goose, whale with a polka dot tail, and so on. Let the children make up verses.

Catalina Magnalina

She had a peculiar name, but she wasn't to blame.
She got it from her mother, who's the same, same, same.

Chorus:
Catalina Magnalina Hootensteiner Bogentwiner
Hogan Logan Bogan was her name.

She had two peculiar teeth in her mouth,
One pointed north, and the other pointed south.
(Chorus)

She had two peculiar eyes in her head,
One was purple, and the other was red.
(Chorus)

Add your own verses.

> BY LAUGHING, YOU CAN BOOST BOTH YOUR MIND AND YOUR BODY.

Tooty Ta

(Chant this as you follow the directions below.)

Chorus: (Clap hands overhead.)

A tooty ta, A tooty ta.
A tooty ta ta.
A tooty ta,
A tooty ta.
A tooty ta ta.

Thumbs up. (Stick your thumbs up in front of you each time you say this line.)

Chorus
Thumbs up
Elbows back (Move your elbows back each time you say this line.)

Chorus
Thumbs up
Elbows back
Feet apart (Extend your feet each time you say this line.)

Chorus
Thumbs up
Elbows back
Feet apart
Knees together (Put your knees together each time you say this line.)

Chorus
Thumbs up
Elbows back
Feet apart
Knees together
Tongue out (Stick out your tongue each time you say this line.)

Chorus
Thumbs up
Elbows back
Feet apart
Knees together

Chorus
Thumbs up
Elbows back
Feet apart
Knees together
Tongue out
Turn around (Turn around.)

Chorus

ACCORDING TO RESEARCHERS, LAUGHTER AND HAVING FUN CAN ALSO BOOST THE BODY'S IMMUNE SYSTEM…

…(THROUGH THE PRODUCTION OF INTERLEUKINS) FOR AS LONG AS THREE DAYS

☐ Read humorous books such as *Once upon MacDonald's Farm* by Stephen Gammel, *Caps for Sale* by Esphyr Slobodkina, *Moira's Birthday* by Robert Munsch, *Thomas' Snowsuit* by Robert Munsch, and *Wacky Wednesday* by Theodore LeSieg.

- Support and encourage children's natural clowning around. Try not to be too quick to stop behavior that really is not causing any harm. A quick laugh will reduce stress and boost learning.
- Laugh at yourself when you do something silly. Laugh with children when they do something silly.
- Use humor. Wear roller skates one day. Invite children to work puzzles under a table. Create a tunnel out of boxes and place it at the front door so that the children will have to crawl through the tunnel to get out of the classroom. Wear a clown nose one day.
- Play What If' by asking the children questions. *What if pigs could fly? What if your family pet was an elephant? What if children were in charge of parents?*
- Share appropriate cartoons with children. Read the funny papers with children.
- Share personal stories about funny things.

A QUICK LAUGH WILL REDUCE STRESS AND BOOST LEARNING.

Experiences and Activities for School-Age Children
- Provide joke books for children to read.
- Encourage the children to make up their own jokes.
- Challenge the children to tickle themselves. This actually cannot be done. Apparently for tickling to work, the brain needs tension and surprise. When a child tickles herself, she knows exactly what will happen, eliminating any tension or surprise. How the brain uses this information about tension and surprise is still a mystery to researchers.

Ideas to Use with
Two or More Children

- Try tummy ticklers. Have the children lie on the floor, placing their heads on other children's tummies. Invite the children to start laughing. The children will soon discover that laughing is contagious, and everyone will soon be giggling.
- Play You Can't Make Me Laugh. Sit in a circle. Select one child to be "It." It stands in the center of the circle and tries to make the other children laugh. The child who laughs first becomes the new It.

Books for Infants and Toddlers

The Belly Button Book by Sandra Boynton

Peek-a-Boo by Francesca Ferri

Where Is Baby's Belly Button? by Karen Kratz

Books for Preschool Children

Imogene's Antlers by David Small

Muddle Cuddle by Laurel Dee Gugler

Silly Sally by Audrey Wood

Books for School-Age Children

Diary of a Wimpy Kid series by Jeff Kinney

Funny Stories for 6 Year Olds by Helen Paiba

Where the Sidewalk Ends by Shel Silverstein

Want to Read More?

Chudler, E. 2012. Laughter and the brain. *Neuroscience for Kids*.
http://faculty.washington.edu/chudler/laugh.html

Jensen. E. 2008. *Brain-based learning: The new paradigm of teaching.* New York: Corwin Press.

Kuwana, E. 2001. The science of laughter. *Neuroscience for Kids*.
http://faculty.washington.edu/chudler/scilaugh.html

Provine, R. R. 2000. *Laughter. A scientific investigation.* New York: Viking.

Warner, J. 2003. Funny thing about humor and the brain: Humor activates reward center of the brain, posted March 31, 2004, *Beating the beast: An online depression support community.*
ww.beatingthebeast.com/forum/index.php?showtopic=3324

I Hear!
I See!
I Do!

CHAPTER TEN

LEARNING STYLES
AND THE BRAIN

Researchers have long been baffled by their inability to prove that matching the delivery of information to a child's learning style enhances learning. Doing so has been treated as a truism in much of recent educational theory and practice. However, new findings from neuroscience point out that children display different learning styles in different situations (Scott et al., 2010). A child may exhibit one style while putting a puzzle together and a completely different style while participating in a music activity. This information does not mean that learning styles are not important; as a matter of fact, it shows how important it is to address all learning styles in each learning experience.

LEARNING STYLES

Auditory learners use listening and speaking to activate learning. Examples of activities that may encourage learners to use their auditory learning style as a dominant stimulus for learning are listening to a story, participating in class discussions, singing songs, painting to music, playing musical instruments, and following verbal directions.

Visual learners use visual images to activate learning. Examples of activities that may encourage learners to use their visual learning style as a dominant stimulus for learning are drawing, painting, looking at a book, determining a framework for a block structure, or putting together a puzzle.

Kinesthetic learners use body movement to engage the brain in learning. Examples of activities that may encourage learners to use their kinesthetic learning style as a dominant stimulus for learning are exercising, dancing, outdoor play, building, painting, modeling with clay, finger painting, and story re-enactment.

Ideas for Using Learning Styles to Boost Brain Power

Experiences and Activities for Infants and Toddlers

In general, infants and toddlers do not display learning styles, although they are developing preferences for approaching their learning opportunities. Their sensory systems are functioning at peak levels. They are using all of their senses as they explore the environment. As often as possible provide auditory, visual, and kinesthetic experiences for little ones. Interact with children as they explore. Ask questions and add comments about their actions. This will add an auditory piece to their tactile and visual exploration.

Experiences and Activities for Preschool Children

☐ Spend less time focusing on "matching" teaching to learning styles and more time on setting high expectations for all children and providing the motivation and skills necessary to attain them. Instead of trying to present a story in a variety of different formats to meet different learning styles, focus on helping children comprehend the plot of the story by asking "thinking questions." For example, you might say, "Goldilocks went into the bears' house uninvited, and she broke a chair. This story is a make-believe story so we know it didn't really happen. What would happen to Goldilocks if she went into a house in your neighborhood uninvited and broke a chair?"

AUDITORY LEARNERS USE LISTENING AND SPEAKING TO ACTIVATE LEARNING.

Start Smart, Revised

- Include strategies that appeal to each learning style (visual, auditory, and kinesthetic) during group activities and instruction.
- Encourage children to verbalize their thinking. Preschool children do not have internal talk like older children. Helping preschool children put their thinking into words reinforces what they are learning. It also adds an auditory element to visual and kinesthetic activities.
- For most learning activities, it is best to start with concrete examples and then move to the verbal and visual explanations.

Experiences and Activities for School-Age Children

- Discuss learning styles with the children. Encourage them to keep journals describing how they approach the things they are learning. After a few weeks of making journal entries, ask the children to review the learning styles they used for various activities. Ask the children questions about whey they see in their journal entries. *Do the children see a pattern? Do they depend on one style more often than another? Does one style work better than another?*
- Challenge the children to write a song that includes hand movements and then perform their song for an audience.

Ideas to Use with Two or More Children

- Encourage the children to participate in a play. Invite them to help select a script (or create one), develop the props, try out for parts, and do all the other aspects of the performance. After the performance, challenge children to reflect on how they used different learning styles in the various stages of the project.
- Assign a project to a small group of children. For example, ask the group to prepare a

VISUAL LEARNERS USE VISUAL IMAGES TO ACTIVATE LEARNING.

KINESTHETIC LEARNERS USE BODY MOVEMENT TO ENGAGE THE BRAIN IN LEARNING.

recipe or to build a structure with blocks using a plan. Have the group think about how they use auditory, visual, and kinesthetic skills as they work. Discuss the children's findings when they conclude their project.

☐ After reading a story, have the children re-enact it. This activity appeals to all learning styles. Discuss which learning styles the children use during the different parts of the re-enactment.

Books for Infants and Toddlers

I Hear by Helen Oxenbury
I See by Helen Oxenbury
I Touch by Helen Oxenbury

Books for Preschool Children

Listen to the Rain by Bill Martin, Jr.
Max Found Two Sticks by Brian Pinkney
Ten Black Dots by Donald Crews
Silly Sally by Audrey Wood

Books for School-Age Children

Celebrating Chinese New Year by Diane Hoyt-Goldsmith
The Dancing Dragon by Marcia K. Vaughan

Want to Read More?

Jensen, E. 2008. *Brain-based learning: The new paradigm of teaching.* New York: Corwin Press.

Scott, L. O., Lynn, S. J., Ruscio, J., & Beyerstein, B. L. 2010. *50 Great myths of popular psychology: Shattering widespread misconceptions about human behavior.* Hoboken, NJ: Wiley-Blackwell.

CHAPTER ELEVEN

Touch, Toss, Turn, Twirl

MOVEMENT AND THE BRAIN

Early movement experiences build neural connections in children's brains. Balance, manipulation, rhythms, midline activities, vestibular activities, and perceptual-sensory activities (combining vision and tactile engagement) all assist learning. "Physical activity stimulates the body to create a hormone that acts like Miracle-Gro for the brain." (Ratley, 2009)

The developing brain uses incoming sensory, perceptual, and movement information to forge its wiring and connections. Consistent, repeated, and multi-sensory learning experiences strengthen brain network connections. These learning experiences develop the brain's cognitive understanding and increase its ability to retrieve information in new situations.

The ability to control the movement of opposite sides and different parts of the body at the same time is actually a learned skill that children

> CONSISTENT, REPEATED, AND MULTISENSORY LEARNING EXPERIENCES STRENGTHEN BRAIN NETWORK CONNECTIONS.

develop over time. Preschool children find it difficult to reach across the body with the right hand to reach something on the left—to cross the body's midline. As children learn to make both sides of the body work together, new pathways between the left and right hemispheres of the brain are created.

We use gestures when explaining a complex topic, but we also move our hands while simply talking with a friend. These spontaneous hand movements are not random—they reflect our thoughts (Goldin-Meadow, 2010). Children who are on the verge of mastering a task reflect this in their gestures. Sensitive teachers and caregivers can glean information from these exaggerated movements, and often do so unconsciously.

When children exercise, they are building muscle, and they are boosting brainpower. Neuroscientist Henriette van Praag and her colleagues at the National Institute on Aging in Bethesda, Maryland, among dozens of other teams of researchers, have discovered that exercise increases key proteins that help build the brain's infrastructure for learning and memory (2009).
* Additional research on page 169 in the Appendix.

Ideas to Enhance Learning with Movement

Experiences and Activities for Infants and Toddlers

☐ Sit with baby in your lap so the baby is facing a mirror. Exercise the baby's arms and legs while he watches himself in the mirror.

☐ Add some paint to the fun! Place a large sheet of paper and fingerpaints on the floor. Invite the children to get on their hands and knees and paint on the sheet of paper. This activity will strengthen children's shoulders and hips and will encourage them to shift their weight.

☐ Provide balls made of different materials for the children to explore for additional sensory input.

- Blow bubbles. Have the children try to pop the bubbles.
- Provide soft blocks or paper-bag blocks for children to stack and then kick or knock down. To make paper-bag blocks, fill large paper grocery bags three-quarters full with crumpled newspaper. Fold the tops of the bags down to create cubes, and then use heavy-duty tape to secure the tops.
- Place contact paper on the floor with its sticky side facing up. Hold the child's hand while he or she touches the paper with his or her foot, or tries to walk on the paper with your help and supervision.
- Make a "mountain" out of blankets, pillows, or carpet squares. Encourage little ones to crawl over the mountain.
- Crawl around the floor with babies. Stop occasionally and rock back and forth. Rocking encourages the development of the vestibular area of the brain, which is responsible for balance and coordination.

Experiences and Activities for Preschool Children
- Ask children to pose in statue positions and hold their poses to the count of five. Change positions and count again. As a variation, stand in a pose and have the children copy that pose.
- Play the following game:

Hello! My Name Is Joe!
Hello! My name is Joe!
I have a wife, one kid, and I work in a button factory.
One day, my boss said, "Are you busy?"
I said, "No."
"Then turn a button with your right hand."
(Make turning gesture with right hand.)

Hello! My name is Joe!
I have a wife, two kids, and I work in a button factory.
One day, my boss said, "Are you busy?"
I said, "No."
"Then turn a button with your left hand."
(Make turning gesture with left hand as you continue with the right hand.)

EXERCISE BUILDS MUSCLES AND BOOSTS BRAINPOWER.

Continue adding number of children and adding right and left feet and head.

Hello! My name is Joe!
I have a wife, six kids, and I work in a button factory.
One day, my boss said, "Are you busy?"
I said, "Yes!"

☐ Observe children's gestures. Exaggerated movements often foretell a breakthrough in understanding. Continue interacting with and encouraging the child until she masters the skill on which she is working.

☐ Place bulletin-board paper low on the wall and have children paint on the paper while on their knees. This will help exercise the children's arms and hips. For a variation, have the children take off their shoes and lie on their backs. Challenge the children to paint with their feet.

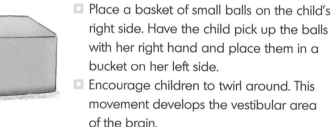

☐ Bring balls outside for the children to kick and play with.

☐ Hang a tetherball from a tree limb that is slightly above the height of the children. Encourage the children to jump up and hit the ball with their hands.

☐ Create an obstacle course for children to navigate. Use rope, Hula Hoops, cones, discarded tires, and/or boxes. Have the children run through the maze, crawl through the maze, or ride a tricycle through the maze.

☐ Place a basket of small balls on the child's right side. Have the child pick up the balls with her right hand and place them in a bucket on her left side.

☐ Encourage children to twirl around. This movement develops the vestibular area of the brain.

Experiences and Activities for School-Age Children

- Encourage children to run laps, increasing distance over time.
- Teach children how to play Ping-Pong or badminton. Both games are active and use cross-lateral movements.
- Encourage children to learn "fad dances" such as the Macarena, the Chicken Dance, the macarena, or the Twist.

Ideas to Use with Two or More Children

- Organize some team sports for the children.
- Suggest that children play traditional group games such as Red Light, Green Light; Simon Says; and Mother May I?

See the chapters on exercise (pages 49–54), small muscles (pages 145–152) and cross-lateral movements (paged 31–40) for additional activities.

Books for Infants and Toddlers

Head to Toe by Eric Carle
Head, Shoulders, Knees, and Toes by Annie Kubler

Books for Preschool Children

Amazing Grace by Mary Hoffman
Baby Dance by Ann Taylor
Dance, Tanya by Patricia Lee Gauch
Eight Animals Bake a Cake by Susan Middleton Elya

Books for School-Age Children

Enemy Pie by Derek Munson
Frank Was a Monster Who Wanted to Dance by Keith Graves

AS CHILDREN LEARN TO MAKE BOTH SIDES OF THE BODY WORK TOGETHER, NEW PATHWAYS …BETWEEN THE LEFT AND RIGHT HEMISPHERES OF THE BRAIN ARE CREATED.

Want to Read More?

Goldin-Meadow, S. 2010, Hands in the air. *Scientific American Mind.* 21, 49–55.

Hannaford, C. 2007. *Smart moves: Why learning is not all in your head,* revised. Salt Lake City, UT: Great Rivers Publications.

Ratey, J. & Hagerman, E. 2008. *Spark: The revolutionary new science of exercise and the brain.* New York: Little, Brown and Company.

Start with a Song

MUSIC AND THE BRAIN

All early sounds, including music and rhythms, play an important role in shaping the brain. The latest research data show that music and language are so intertwined that an awareness of music is critical to a baby's language development (Deutsch, 2010). As children grow, music may foster their communication skills. Understanding the structure of songs helps children learn to talk, read, and even make friends.

Brain areas governing music and language overlap. Music and language have much in common. Both are governed by rules and basic elements (words and notes). In language, words make phrases that combine to make clauses and eventually sentences. In music, notes combine and grow to form a melody.

Speech has a natural melody called *prosody*. Prosody is the rhythmic and intonational aspect of language. It changes with emotions. The more excited the speaker, the faster the rhythm. It also emphasizes word boundaries. Prosody is exaggerated in the way people speak to infants. This high pitch sing song language is referred to as *parentese*.

The neural pathways between language and music are also influenced by a person's native language. A repetition of notes may sound different to a person whose native language is English than it will sound to a person whose native language is Chinese. All languages have a "melody" that is unique. Infants echo the inherent melodies of their native language when they cry, long before they speak.

The term *Mozart effect* comes from a study (Shaw & Leng, 1988) whose results seemed to indicate that listening to the music of Mozart can have a positive effect on brain activity. Subsequent studies have shown that this effect, although we still hear it mentioned frequently, does not appear to have any solid basis in research (Steele, Bass, & Crook, 1999).

Love for, response to and appreciation of music is a universal feature of human culture. It has been suggested that music predates language. There is no question that music is an important part of human life. Researchers can verify and quantify emotional responses to music (Steidl, et al., 2006), and that emotions boost memory (Zald, 2003).

* Additional research on pages 169–171 in the Appendix.

Ideas for Using Music to Support Language and to Stimulate Alertness

Experiences and Activities for
Infants and Toddlers

- ☐ Sing, sing, sing to newborn children.
- ☐ Use "parentese" with infants.
  - ☐ Play a variety of music CDs (classical, country, jazz, pop) for babies. **Warning:** Make sure that the volume is low. Young ears are sensitive to sound.

- Hold babies in your arms and dance to music. Encourage toddlers to dance with you.
- Invite toddlers to march to music. Provide music makers or rhythm band instruments so little ones can help make music.
- Give toddlers the opportunity to make music. Provide rattles or pots for children to experiment with sounds. Demonstrate and encourage children to copy you. Add to the complexity of your musical pattern as babies and toddlers catch on to the game.

Experiences and Activities for Preschool Children

- Sing a song—any song—every morning to start the day.
- Use songs to introduce information to children. For example, use "Itsy Bitsy Spider" (page 34) to introduce information about spiders; "Twinkle, Twinkle, Little Star" (page 43) to explore nighttime; and "Rain, Rain, Go Away" to begin a discussion about weather.

Rain, Rain, Go Away
Rain, rain, go away
Come again some other day.
We want to go out and play,
Come again some other day.

- Play marching music and invite children to create different marching steps (high steps, fast steps, long steps).
- Play a xylophone. Challenge children to stand up as the notes go up the scale and sit down as the notes go down the scale.
- Provide streamers or scarves for the children to move with and explore as they listen to the rhythm of music.
- Make homemade band instruments. For example, rubber bands and a shoebox make a great guitar, paper plates and kernels of popcorn make a good maraca, a spoon and a pie pan make a cymbal, and a stick and a box make a drum.
- Provide musical instruments for exploration. Xylophones, piano keyboards, autoharps, and drums are all intriguing to children and great for exploring notes, tones, and chords.

EXPLORE DIFFERENT TYPES OF MUSIC WITH CHILDREN.

- Provide books based on songs, such as *The Wheels on the Bus* by Raffi and *Itsy Bitsy Spider* by Iza Trapani.
- Invite children to listen to a variety of music and then ask the children to select music for the background of a story. For example, use scary music for when the wolf comes to the doors of the three pigs and happy music when the pigs are safe.
- Schedule a special music appreciation time a couple of times each week. Explore different types of music with the children.
- Model a love for music. Individuals who truly love music listen to it more and, therefore, enjoy the positive effects associated with music.

Experiences and Activities for School-Age Children

- Invite the children to turn traditional tales into musical plays. "The Three Billy Goats Gruff" and "The Three Little Pigs" both work well.
- Encourage the children to try an experiment: Listen to Mozart before working puzzles or before a thinking activity like brainstorming. Ask, *Do you feel smarter after listening to Mozart's music?*
- Sing "The Alphabet Song" and "Twinkle, Twinkle, Little Star" with the children. Ask them how the songs are alike (they have the same tune) and how they are different (they have different words).
- Take children on field trips to symphonies and operas that are appropriate. Many places offer special performances just for children.
- Take the children on a field trip to hear a high school band or orchestra. Before or after the performance, arrange for a visit with the performers and their instruments. If possible, have the children sit among the musicians.

Start Smart, Revised

Later on, ask the children, *Does the music sound different when you are in the middle of the instruments?*

Ideas to Use with Two or More Children

- Challenge children to create a musical talent show.
- Play some music that the children like, and invite them to perform a mirror dance. Have each child select a partner. Partners take turns being the leader and the follower. The leader creates moves, and the follower copies the movements.
- Play some bright, rhythmic music. Stand facing a child (or partner two children) and point out the different parts of the legs and feet. Encourage the child to explore all the ways each part can move: bend the knees, wiggle the toes, circle the ankles, arch the foot, kick, and hop. Have the children dance on one leg and then dance with both legs. When the children are ready, add other parts of the body—head, arms, shoulders, back, and waist.
- Play Musical Ball Pass. Pass a ball while music is playing. When the music stops, the child holding the ball sits down. Continue passing the ball until only one child remains standing. (Encourage the children to try funny ways to pass the ball such as between their legs, over their heads, behind their backs).
- Play Musical Hide and Seek. Select a child to be It. Ask It to leave the room, and then hide an object like a ball or a beanbag somewhere in the room. When It returns, have the children start singing a song. The children should sing loudly when It is near the object and softly when It is not close to the object. Continue until It finds the object.
- Roll a ball to music. Have children sit in a circle and spread their legs until their toes are touching their neighbors' toes on each side. Play some music and have the children roll a ball to each other following the tempo of the music. Try music with different tempos.
- Use songs during transitions. Here are two suggestions:

Clean-Up Time (Tune: "Here We Go 'Round the Mulberry Bush")
This is the way we clean the room, clean the room, clean the room.
This is the way we clean the room, so early in the morning (or, before we go outside).

Snack or Meal Time (Tune: "The More We Get Together")
The more we get together, together, together,
The more we get together, the happier are we!

Books for Infants and Toddlers

Itsy Bitsy Spider by Iza Trapani
Twinkle, Twinkle, Little Star by Iza Trapani

Books for Preschool Children

Bremen Town Musicians—many versions available
Down by the Bay by Raffi
Froggie Went A-Courting by Chris Conover
I Like the Music by Leah Komaiko
Lullabies and Night Songs by William Engvick
Old MacDonald Had a Farm by Robert M. Quackenbush
Wheels on the Bus by Raffi

Books for School-Age Children

The Birthday Ball by Lois Lowry
The Jazz Fly by Matthew Gollub
Zin! Zin! Zin! A Violin by Lloyd Moss

Start Smart, Revised

Want to Read More?

Deutsch, D. 2010. Speaking in tones. *Scientific American Mind*. 21 (3): 36–43.

Heslet, L. 2003. Our musical brain. *Musica Humana*.
   http;//www.musicahumana.org/documents/00076.pdf.

Levintin, D. J. & Tiroolas, A. K. 2009. Current advances in the cognitive neuroscience
   of music. *The year in cognitive neuroscience 2009*. New York Academy of
   Sciences, Miller, M. & Kingstone, A., eds. 1156: 211–231.

Leng, X., Shaw, G. L., & Wright, E. L. 1990. Coding of musical structure and the trion
   model of cortex. *Music Perception*, 8: 49-62.

Parbery-Clark, A., Skoe, E., & Kraus, K. 2009. Music and the brain. *The Journal of
   Neuroscience* 29 (45): 14100–14107.

Parbery-Clark, A., Skoe, E., Lam, C., & Kraus, N. 2009. Musician enhancement for
   speech-in-noise. *Ear & Hearing* 30(6): 653–661.

Rauscher F. H., Shaw, G. L., & Ky, K. N. 1993. Music and spatial task performance.
   Nature 365: 611.

Steele, K. M., Bass, K. E., & Crook, M. D. 1999. The mystery of the Mozart effect:
   Failure to replicate. *Psychological Science*. 10: 366–369.

Steidl, S., Mohiuddin, S., & Anderson, A. 2006. Effects of emotional
   arousal on multiple memory systems: Evidence from declarative
   and procedural learning. *Learning and Memory*, 13, 650–658.

Zald, D.H. 2003. The human amygdala and the emotional
   evaluation of sensory stimuli. *Brain Research: Brain Research
   Reviews*. 41, 88–123.

IN LANGUAGE, WORDS MAKE PHRASES THAT COMBINE TO MAKE CLAUSES AND EVENTUALLY SENTENCES.

IN MUSIC, NOTES COMBINE AND GROW TO FORM A MELODY.

Start Smart, Revised

The Power of New

NOVELTY AND THE BRAIN

The brain pays close attention to things that do not fit an established pattern, things that are new, and things that are different. What the brain is accustomed to becomes routine and, over time, the brain reacts to a routine stimulus by lowering the level of activity. Anything new causes the body to release adrenaline, and adrenaline acts as both a memory fixative and a stimulus for alertness (Bunzeck and Düzel, 2006).

Researchers have found additional brain benefits to novelty. Novelty stimulates activity in a number of brain systems, especially the dopamine system. This system, which is deep in the brain stem, sends the neurotransmitter dopamine to locations across the brain. Many people incorrectly think of dopamine as the "feel-good" neurotransmitter because drugs that create euphoria cause an increase of dopamine in particular parts of the brain. However, a growing body of new research shows that dopamine acts as an "I want more" neurotransmitter (Joseph, 2008).

* Additional research on page 172 in the Appendix.

ANYTHING NEW CAUSES THE BODY TO RELEASE ADRENALINE. ADRENALINE ACTS AS

BOTH A MEMORY FIXATIVE AND A STIMULUS FOR ALERTNESS (BUNZECK AND DÜZEL, 2006).

CHAPTER THIRTEEN

Ideas for Using Novelty to Stimulate Learning (Alertness and Memory)

Experiences and Activities for Infants and Toddlers

- ☐ Wear a funny hat or large sunglasses while changing a baby's diaper. Talk with the baby about your hat or glasses.
- ☐ Change the seating arrangements for lunch time. Point out the changes. Note which aspects of the arrangement are different, such as the direction the child is facing, which children now sit next to each other, and the different views the children have in the new seating arrangement.
- ☐ From time to time, rotate toys and mobiles in the play area.
- ☐ At the changing table, place the child in a new position (head at opposite end). Make sure the new position is safe.

Experiences and Activities for Preschool Children

- ☐ Rearrange the children's toys and equipment every so often. Let the children help if they express an interest in doing so. **Note:** Be sure the children are ready for this; too much change can be upsetting.
- ☐ Rotate the toys in the children's play area. Put some things away for a couple of months, and then bring them out again. Also rotate books on the library shelf.
- ☐ Challenge the children to work puzzles with the pieces upside down. Have the children string beads on pieces of yarn that hang from the ceiling. Challenge the children to ride tricycles or bicycles backwards.
- ☐ Tape paper under a table or to a window, and invite the children to color on the paper with crayons or markers.
  - ☐ Cut easel paper into creative shapes for the children to draw or paint on.

- Follow the daily routine backwards one day. Children really get a kick out of this, especially if you tie it to the book *Wacky Wednesday* by Theodore LeSieg.
- Create new verses to songs, and sing old ones to different tunes. Try singing "Itsy Bitsy Spider" (page 34) to the tune of "Twinkle, Twinkle, Little Star" (page 43) and vice versa.
- Combine things in unexpected ways. Try putting the dishes with the blocks or Legos with art supplies. Stand back and watch how the children incorporate these items in their play.
- Read a book backwards. Sometimes it still makes sense. Try *Brown Bear, Brown Bear, What Do You See?* Try one that won't make sense, such as *Strega Nona* by Tomie dePaola or *The Very Hungry Caterpillar* by Eric Carle.
- Serve the children hot dogs for breakfast and pancakes for lunch.
- Bring the children outside or to another room for snack or lunch. Make it a picnic.
- Switch roles with the children. Let them read to you or decide what to eat.
- Encourage the children to nap with their heads at the opposite ends of their mats.
- Take a walk in the neighborhood. Try walking backwards.

Experiences and Activities for School-Age Children

- Encourage the children to examine a current event from the perspective of someone from another country, another planet, or another time in history.

NOVELTY STIMULATES ACTIVITY IN A NUMBER OF BRAIN SYSTEMS, ESPECIALLY THE DOPAMINE SYSTEM.

NEW RESEARCH SHOWS THAT DOPAMINE ACTS AS

AN "I WANT MORE" NEUROTRANSMITTER.

- Invite children to try new projects that they have not previously tried such as designing a campaign to clean up the environment or planting a garden.
- Challenge the children to make something useful from a paper plate or cup.
- Invite the children to think of a new ending to *Goldilocks and the Three Bears* and other traditional tales.
- Provide a video camera, and challenge the children to create a documentary.
- Invite the children to make up word scrabbles using their spelling words.
- Challenge the children to search the dictionary for words that have 10 or more letters. Have the children use the words they find in a sentence. This is a great contest!
- Make photocopies of newspaper comic strips. (Block the dialogue boxes before copying.) Encourage the children to write new dialogue for the comic strips.

Ideas to Use with Two or More Children

- Ask the children to change the names of traditional games. For example, Simon Says can become Chuckie Says; Duck, Duck, Goose can be Dog, Dog, Cat; and then have them play the game using the new words.
- Challenge the children to make up new rules for or ways to play games. This could include having players move backwards around a game board or using a spinner-die combination instead of two dice.

Books for Infants and Toddlers

Peep-a-Who by Nina Laden
Pocket Frog by Annie Kubler

Books for Preschool Children

Bored—Nothing to Do! by Peter Spier

The Cat in the Hat by Dr. Seuss

Falling Up by Shel Silverstein

If… by Sarah Perry

Imogene's Antlers by David Small

Jennie's Hat by Ezra Jack Keats

Look Again! by Tana Hoban

Tuesday by David Wiesner

Wacky Wednesday by Theo LeSieg

Books for School-Age Children

This Isn't What It Looks Like by Pseudonymous Bosch

Where the Sidewalk Ends by Shel Silverstein

Want to Read More?

Bunzeck, N. and Düzel, E. 2006. Absolute coding of stimulus novelty in the human substantia. *Neuron.* 51 (3): 369–379.

Joseph, J.E., Liu, X., Jiang, Y., Lynam, D., & Kelly, T.H. 2008. Neural correlates of emotional reactivity in sensation seeking. *Psychological Science* 20 (2), 215–223.

Martin, S.B., Covell, D.J., Joseph, J.E., Chebrolu, H., Smith, C.D., Kelly, T.H., Jiang, Y. & Gold, B.T. 2007. Human experience seeking correlates with hippocampus volume: Convergent evidence from manual tracing and voxel-based morphometry. *Neuropsychologia* 45: 2874–2881.

Perry, B. 2000. How the brain learns best. *Instructor* 6: 34–37.

Zuckerman, M. 2007. *Sensation seeking and risky behavior.* Washington, DC: American Psychological Association.

THE BRAIN PAYS CLOSE ATTENTION TO THINGS THAT ARE NEW AND THINGS THAT ARE DIFFERENT.

Start Smart, Revised

Feeding the Brain

NUTRITION AND THE BRAIN

> THE BRAIN NEEDS GLUCOSE, VITAMINS, MINERALS, AND OTHER ESSENTIAL NUTRIENTS TO FUNCTION EFFECTIVELY.

Good nutrition is fundamental to brain function. The brain needs glucose, vitamins, minerals, and other essential nutrients to function effectively. The brain receives the glucose it needs for energy and the proteins and fats it needs for constructing neural connections from what we eat. Balance is important. Too little of these nutrients or too much of these nutrients can affect the nervous system (Bedi, 2003).

The brain seems to function best when we eat protein, carbohydrates with protein, selenium (seafood, nuts, whole-grain breads), boron (broccoli, apples, peaches, grapes), folic acid (green leafy vegetables, beef liver, beans), zinc (fish, beans, grains), and both vitamin B_{12} and B complex. All of these vitamins and nutrients are more effective when obtained from a natural source as opposed to a supplement.

* Additional research on page 171 in the Appendix.

Ideas for Using Nutrition to Build Brain Power

Experiences and Activities for Infants and Toddlers

☐ Offer healthy snacks for little ones. Even before a child begins speaking, talk to her about what makes the snacks healthy. You are planting the seeds for making healthy food choices. Here are some suggestions for toddlers:

- **Fresh Fruit:** apples, bananas, pears, melon, kiwi, grapes, mango
- **Dried Fruit:** apricots, banana chips, apples, raisins, cranberries, blueberries, cherries, papaya
- **Cheese:** Cut block cheese into squares or offer the prepackaged string cheese sticks.

Safety note: Peel fruit such as apples with tough skins, and cut firm fruit such as grapes into bite-sized pieces. Observe children as they eat to make sure that the food you offer does not pose a choking hazard. As always, check for allergies before serving food to children.

☐ Provide photos of foods and plastic fruit and vegetables for infants and toddlers to explore.

☐ Use encouragement (smile and make positive comments) when infants and toddlers are trying new foods.

Experiences and Activities for Preschool Children

☐ Offer protein-rich snacks such as cheese, yogurt, deviled eggs, nuts, and fruits.

☐ Teach the children about nutrition. Help the children recognize healthy and unhealthy foods and habits.

☐ Set a good example by what you eat. Eat healthy foods and talk with the children about how these foods help keep you healthy.

☐ Try some of the following food-related activities:

- After reading *Green Eggs and Ham* by Dr. Seuss, fix green eggs and ham for the children. To make the eggs green, stir finely shredded parsley or broccoli into the eggs while cooking.
- Invite children to shell peanuts, which is great for fine motor development. After the children finish shelling the peanuts, make peanut butter or just allow the children to eat the peanuts they shelled.
- Dye hard-boiled eggs with natural dyes—purple (beet juice), yellow (tea), green (spinach or broccoli), pink (strawberries), and blue (blueberries). Boil items

SAFETY NOTE: CHECK FOR ALLERGIES BEFORE SERVING FOOD TO CHILDREN.

separately. After boiling each item, reserve the liquid in which it boiled to use as the dyes. When the liquids are cool, show the children the items that produced each color. After dyeing the eggs, serve them for snack.

■ Offer several types of nuts. Invite children to sort the nuts by picking them up with tongs and placing them into the compartments of a muffin tin. After the children sort the nuts, let everyone taste them. Ask the children which nuts are their favorites, and graph the results.

■ Make letter pretzels using the following recipe:

Pretzel Recipe
1½ cups warm water
4 cups wheat flour
1 envelope yeast
1 teaspoon salt
1 egg
coarse salt

Mix the first four ingredients together. Give the children enough dough to shape into the first letters of their names. Brush the dough letters with beaten egg and sprinkle with coarse salt. Bake at 425° F for 12 minutes.
Makes three large letters or four smaller letters.

RECIPE CARD

☐ Make gelatin shapes using the recipe on the next page.

Gelatin Shapes

12 ounces frozen apple or grape juice concentrate (thawed)

3 envelopes unflavored gelatin

1⅔ cups hot water

Mix the ingredients together. Stir well. Pour the mixture into a 9" x 13" pan.
Chill. Cut into shapes or strips.

Note: Check for food allergies before serving any food to children.

- Hungry children have a difficult time focusing and paying attention. Try your own experiment. Provide nibbling items throughout the day. Do you notice any difference in children's level of alertness?
- Discuss My Plate with the children. www.ChooseMyPlate.gov.
- Serve the children breakfast or a healthy morning snack; it starts the brain working. Eggs, yogurt, fruits, whole-grain cereals, and breads are a brain-friendly way to start the day.

Experiences and Activities for School-Age Children

- Plan weekly menus with the children. Discuss healthy choices to include on the menus. Help the children to design balanced meals.
- Take a field trip to a grocery store. Ask the children to locate foods from each food group.
  - Challenge the children to keep a log of their food intake for a week. At the end of the week, discuss what they ate.
    - Help the children plant and maintain a vegetable garden, or if space is limited, plant an herb garden in containers in the classroom. Let the children research the vegetables or herbs. Have them find out the proper planting times and harvest time. Challenge the children to find out the nutritional value of each item they choose to

plant. Be sure to prepare some of the harvest and share it with another class or family.

☐ Help children make Creamy Orange Shakes. Place ½ cup of orange-flavored frozen yogurt in a blender along with ¾ cup of fat-free milk. Blend and serve. Makes two servings.

An Idea to Use with Two or More Children

☐ Create an open snack table. Provide various snacks that the children can have throughout the day. Decide the number of times a child can go to the snack table, and regulate this by using a monitoring system. Try using key tags on a board with cup hooks. Color a happy face on one side and place the child's name on the other side. After the child has a snack, he can turn the key tag over so the happy face is showing. Clothespins with children's names on them could also be used to keep track of visits to the snack table.

Books for Infants and Toddlers

Eating the Rainbow by Rena Grossman
First Words by Louis Weber
Sign About Meal Time by Anthony Lewis

Books for Preschool Children

D.W. The Picky Eater by Marc Brown
Daddy Makes the Best Spaghetti by Anna Grossnickle Hines
Green Eggs and Ham by Dr. Seuss
Growing Vegetable Soup by Lois Ehlert
Now I Will Never Leave the Dinner Table by Jane Read Martin and Patricia Mark
Yucky Yummy by Leslie Patricelli

VITAMINS AND NUTRIENTS ARE MORE EFFECTIVE WHEN OBTAINED FROM A NATURAL SOURCE AS OPPOSED TO A SUPPLEMENT.

Books for School-Age Children

The Cafeteria Lady from the Black Lagoon by Mike Thaler
Where Does Your Food Go? by Wiley Blevens

Want to Read More?

Bedi, K.S. 2003. Nutritional effects on neuron numbers. *Nutritional Neuroscience*. 6 (3): 141–52.

Dauncey, M.J. 2009. New insights into nutrition and cognitive neuroscience. *Proceedings of the Nutrition Society*. 68(4): 408–15.

Mathers J.C. 2007. Early nutrition: impact on epigenetics. *Forum of Nutrition*. 60: 42–48.

Less Is More!

OVER-STIMULATION AND THE BRAIN

CHAPTER FIFTEEN

TYPICALLY, THE BRAIN RECEIVES 35,000–42,000 BITS OF INFORMATION PER SECOND.

Imagine how you might feel in the middle of this scenario:

> You have just gotten home from work. You are trying to get dinner cooking. You open the refrigerator and find pork chops, ground meat, chicken, and pizza. The television is blaring in one room and a CD is playing in another. The phone rings. Your two older children are quarreling, and your toddler is crying because she is hungry and wants a cookie. Someone has left an empty milk carton and various other empty containers and trash on the drain board. Your spouse walks in and asks, "What's for dinner?"

Does just reading this make you anxious? This is overstimulation—too many distractions, clutter, and choices.

The brain is constantly taking in information from the environment. Typically, the brain receives 35,000–42,000 bits of information per second—way too much to absorb. The brain is less like a sponge absorbing this information and more like a filter, working hard to keep all the distracting pieces of information from interfering with the important pieces of information on which it needs to focus (Sousa, 2006).

The brain receives information through the senses: sight, hearing, taste, touch, and smell. Examples include feeling clothing on our skin, sensing the lighting and the temperature in our surroundings, and hearing sounds around us. The brain manages to filter out most of these stimuli, because absorbing all of it at once would be overwhelming to the brain. The senses do not transmit information equally. Sight, hearing, and touch contribute the most information with sight contributing significantly more data than hearing and touch. Researchers suggest that 85 percent of the information the brain registers is from sight, hearing, and touch, with most of that 85 percent from sight alone (Sousa, 1995).

THE BRAIN RECEIVES INFORMATION THROUGH THE SENSES: SIGHT, HEARING, TASTE, TOUCH, AND SMELL.

The brain works hard to filter out unnecessary information so it can focus on important information. The brain's first screening process occurs when nerve endings deliver information to the brain stem. The first thing that the brain does is "close the door" to unnecessary information and "open the door" to relevant information. This process matures over time. Young children's brains are just beginning to develop the ability to filter out irrelevant information.

Too many stimuli can be overwhelming to anyone, but especially to young children whose brains are not as skilled at determining which stimuli to accept and which to reject. Working memory, which has a limited capacity, must process the information that enters the brain. For an adult brain, the capacity of working memory is about seven items. For children younger than five, it is an average of two items, and for children between five and fourteen, it is an average of five (Cowan, 2001). This means that when providing new information to children, it is very important not to overwhelm them with more than they can handle.

Providing too many options to choose from is a form of overstimulation. Too many options overwhelm children and inhibit their ability to make thoughtful choices. Young children do best when they have no more than three choices. For more information about choices, see Chapter 2 on pages 21–24.

Overstimulation interferes with learning, but too little stimulation is also detrimental. The brain develops through the stimulation it receives. Try to maintain a balance that optimizes learning.

Ideas for Eliminating Overstimulation

Experiences and Activities for Infants and Toddlers

- Watch for signs of overstimulation. When an infant arches her back, pulls away, turns her head away, and cries, she is saying, "I've had enough." When toddlers cry, turn away from you, close their eyes, and sometimes when they say no, they are saying they are overwhelmed.
- Provide no more than one or two different toys for each child to explore at any one time.
- Do not give infants and toddlers high-tech materials because these items are often overstimulating and not nearly as effective as simple toys.
- Use simple sentences when talking with children. Avoid talking too much because this diminishes conversation's effectiveness as a teaching tool.
- Limit the amount of wall decoration in your room. One poster (photo or picture) is superior to a collage of photos. Consider changing the posters in your room every few days to keep the children interested in looking for new materials.
- Use transitions when changing from one activity to another. Transitions help reduce overstimulation by allowing children to calm down from one activity before jumping into the next.
- Move slowly through the daily routine. Give little ones time to absorb information and adapt to changes.

Experiences and Activities for Preschool Children

- Reduce the number of wall decorations. Leave some wall space blank. The eye must have a place to rest.
- Instead of labeling everything in the room to create a print-rich environment, label only a few things. Let the children's interests determine which items they would like to see in written form. Keep a recipe box with

labels of all the objects in the classroom, and rotate which objects are labeled at any one time.

☐ Eliminate clutter in the room. Clean off the tops of lockers and bookshelves.

☐ Provide sufficient materials to accommodate the number of children who may be in a specific center of at the same time but do not overdo it. A good rule of thumb is two items more than the number of children the center will accommodate. Rotate the materials over time.

☐ Limit the children's choices to no more than three options of designated games or activities in each center or area. This does not apply to the materials available on shelves or other containers in each center.

Experiences and Activities for School-Age Children

☐ Encourage the children to conduct their own research about the impact of clutter on their ability to focus. Set up two study areas, one that is clutter-free and one that is cluttered. Have children try doing their homework in each area. Which area is more conducive to finishing their homework?

☐ Engage the children in a discussion about stimulation. Talk about forms of stimulation that can be distracting, such as music, loud noises, clutter, cold temperatures, or hot temperatures. Suggest that the children make a list of ways they can eliminate distraction at home and at school.

☐ Invite the children to set up a popcorn stand for younger students. Have the children experiment with offering three flavor choices (plain, with melted butter, with parmesan cheese), and later offer five flavor choices (add with cinnamon sugar, with garlic salt). What happens when more choices are offered?

☐ Encourage school-age children to help decide how to eliminate some of the wall decorations in their space.

Ideas to Use with Two or More Children

- Eliminate wall decorations that do not relate directly to the current instruction. For example, there is no need to put up decorations for shapes, colors, and months of the year if these subjects are not part of the current instruction.
- Select three artists of the week instead of putting every child's artwork up for each art project. This reduces the visual clutter in the classroom.

Books for Infants and Toddlers

Clean-Up Time by Elizabeth Verdick
Hippos Go Berserk! by Sandra Boynton

Books for Preschool Children

Just a Mess by Mercer Mayer
Moira's Birthday by Robert Munsch
Noisy Nora by Rosemary Wells
Too Many Toys by David Shannon
Too Much Noise by Ann McGovern

TOO MANY OPTIONS OVERWHELM CHILDREN AND INHIBIT THEIR ABILITY TO MAKE THOUGHTFUL CHOICES.

Books for School-Age Children

The Kids' Yoga Book of Feelings by Mary Humphrey
Learning to Slow Down and Pay Attention by Kathleen Nadeau and Ellen Dixon

Want to Read More?

Hirsh-Pasek, K. & Golinkoff, R. 2003. *Einstein never used flashcards: How our children really learn and why they need to play more and memorize less.* Emmaus, PA: Rodale Press.

Shore, R. 2003. *Rethinking the brain,* revised. Washington, DC: Families and Work Institute.

Sousa, D. 2005. *How the brain learns,* 3rd edition. New York: Corwin Press.

Sousa, D. 1996. *How the brain learns.* Reston, VA: The National Association of Secondary School Principals.

CHAPTER SIXTEEN

More than Plaids

PATTERNS
AND THE BRAIN

The brain thrives on making and detecting patterns. The human brain is not organized or designed for linear, one-path thought. Instead, it operates by going down many paths simultaneously. The brain compiles information from many sources to determine size, shape, color, texture, weight, smell, movement, and so forth. The brain is constantly making sense out of many bits of information. During the process of making sense of data, the brain is in a state of confusion. During this state of confusion (part of information processing) the brain compares new information to existing information. In other words, it examines similarities and differences (patterns). When the brain makes sense of and establishes meaning for the new information (accommodates the differences), it sends the information to long-term memory (the unconscious level of knowledge). The brain is now ready to move on to the next challenge. When sense and meaning are established, the stage is set for more challenges. Every pattern that the brain is able to create allows it to store that new understanding to long-term memory.

THE BRAIN IS CONSTANTLY MAKING SENSE OUT OF MANY BITS OF INFORMATION.

Multiple intelligence theory suggests that the ability to recognize patterns and build new relationships from the patterns is the essence of intelligence (Gardner, 1981). Helping children to see patterns in language, logic, behaviors, habits, music, body movements, nature, and space may be an important aspect of teaching.

Ideas for Using Patterns to Enhance Long-Term Memory

Experiences and Activities for Infants and Toddlers

☐ Because the primary pattern that infants and toddlers experience is cause and effect, point out cause-and-effect patterns to babies. For example, shaking a rattle harder makes a louder noise than shaking a rattle softly, pushing a button on a toy makes the music start, and smiling brings a smile in return.

☐ Music is full of patterns. Sing songs to children of every age.

☐ Place a variety of toys in front of little ones, and point out how they are similar and how they are different.

☐ Teach the children simple exercises with patterned movements such as toe touches. Speak as you move: *Bend down, touch your toes, stand up. Bend down, touch your toes, stand up….*

Experiences and Activities for Preschool Children

☐ Challenge the children to look for visual patterns in the environment such as shadows on the floor, lines in the carpet, window arrangement in buildings, and so on. Ask the children questions about their observations, such as, *Does the vacuum cleaner create a pattern on the rug? Does the lawn mower create a pattern on the grass? Is there a common cause to each pattern?* Point out the patterns to children and encourage them to look for patterns on their own.

- Whenever possible, point out to the children how new information is similar to existing information. For example, when talking about snakes, point out the similarities snakes have with other reptiles that the children know about, such as turtles and lizards.
- Read the children books and stories that have a repetitive pattern in the language of the text, such as *Brown Bear, Brown Bear, What Do You See?* by Bill Martin, Jr. and any traditional version of *The Three Little Pigs.*
- Read the children stories that have a repetitive pattern in the action, such as *The Three Billy Goats Gruff* (trip-trapping across the bridge) and *The Gingerbread Man* (running away).
- Challenge the children to find patterns in numbers such as odd and even, counting by twos, fives, tens, or adding on one.
- Sing! Songs generally have a pattern—a verse that is repeated or lines that end with rhyming words. Point out the patterns in songs. Songs that have a pattern include "This Old Man" and "Head, Shoulders, Knees, and Toes." Challenge the children to make up new songs with a pattern.

This Old Man
This old man, he played one,
He played knick-knack on my thumb.
With a knick-knack paddy-whack, give your dog a bone.
This old man came rolling home.

This old man, he played two,
He played knick-knack on my shoe…

Three…on my knee	*Seven…up in heaven*
Four…on my door	*Eight…on my gate*
Five…on my hive	*Nine…on my spine*
Six…on my sticks	*Ten…once again*

MUSIC IS FULL OF PATTERNS.

Head, Shoulders, Knees, and Toes
Head, shoulders, knees and toes, knees and toes,
Head, shoulders, knees and toes, knees and toes,
And eyes and ears and mouth and nose.
Head, shoulders, knees and toes, knees and toes.

- Encourage children to create patterns when painting. For example, the children could paint using the following patterns: thin line/thick line, red circle/blue circle, line/dot, color/no color.
- Show the children how to weave crepe paper into the sides of a plastic laundry basket or milk crate, weave construction paper mats, weave on a loom, or weave crepe paper in a chain link fence. Point out color patterns, space patterns, and the over/under movement patterns to the children.
- Do simple repetitive dances, or help them create new dances that have repetitive patterns.
- Create clapping patterns with the children. Let the children record their patterns, then play the children's patterns back to them.

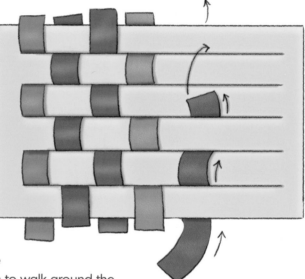

- Talk with the children about the cyclical pattern of seasons, months of the year, and days of the week. Write the months of the year on paper plates. Arrange the plates in a circle on the floor and invite the children to walk around the circle as they recite the months.
- Engage the children in a discussion about school days and weekend days. Ask the children questions, such as, *How are they alike? How are they different? What patterns do you notice in each type of day? How are the patterns alike? How are they different?*
- Understanding cause and effect helps the brain make sense of information. Provide opportunities for children to explore the relationship between cause and effect. Encourage children to rub their hands together and then discuss what happens. Have the children sand a piece of wood and observe

January

December

February

November

March

October

April

September

May

August

June

July

what happens. What happens when the children rub sticks together or rub porous rocks together? Is the effect always the same?

- Provide a kaleidoscope. Talk with the children about the patterns they see.
- Sorting is one step in finding or creating patterns. During snack or lunch time, challenge the children to sort their food by taste. Ask the children, *Which foods taste sweet? Which have a sour taste?*
- Talk about the children's daily routines, such as brushing their teeth after meals and picking up their toys after they are finished playing. Help the children see the repeating pattern of the routines that are part of their daily lives.
- Invite the children to participate in activities that have a pattern, such as putting away blocks or setting the table for snack.
- Help the children identify patterns in clothing such as stripes, dots, and plaids.

Experiences and Activities for School-Age Children
- Play classical music and ask the children what patterns they hear in the music.
- Point out how our bodies have their own patterns—the in-and-out motion of breathing, the rhythm of our heartbeats.
- Suggest that the children observe patterns in the weather. Ask the children, *How could we use the patterns we notice to predict the weather?*
- Help the children find patterns in nature, such as how frost forms in crystals on the windowpane, how water ripples in a puddle, the way bark grows on a tree trunk, the structure of tree branches against the sky, the locations where ferns grow, which side of a tree moss grows on, or the rhythms the rain makes.
- Invite children to solve mental puzzles that involve recognizing patterns. See http://kids.aol.com/games/brain-games.

Ideas to Use with Two or More Children
- Provide children with 4" square sheets of colored cellophane. Invite them to go outside in the sunlight and work together to create a pattern on the ground by letting the sun shine through their sheets of cellophane.
- Suggest that the children watch for patterns in their behaviors. Discuss the patterns by asking the children, *Isn't it interesting that friends are more willing to share when you*

HELP CHILDREN FIND PATTERNS IN NATURE

ask them nicely? Notice how everyone gets a little cranky around lunchtime? How many people are tired after lunch?

□ Play games with patterns, such as Duck, Duck Goose, Hide and Seek, or Musical Chairs. Compare Musical Chairs with Cooperative Musical Chairs (below). Challenge children to find the patterns.

Cooperative Musical Chairs

This game is a variation of Musical Chairs. Place chairs back to back in a line with one fewer chair than there are children playing the game. (This game works best if there are eight or fewer children.) Play a piece of music. The children walk around the chairs until the music stops. When the music stops everyone sits in a chair. The children should share their chairs so no one is left out. The idea is to get everyone on a chair so everyone wins. Remove a chair and go again. The game becomes more amusing as the children try to fit into fewer and fewer chairs. Continue playing for as long as the children are interested.

□ Challenge the children to create patterns using their bodies. For example, one child faces forward, one backward, one forward, and so on. Invite children to create new patterns. Create patterns using criteria that are difficult to recognize (long hair/short hair or freckles/no freckles). Challenge other children to figure out what these patterns are.

□ Use word maps to help children see patterns of relationships. For example, if the children are learning about sea life, let them tell you everything they know about sea life before the lesson begins. Write *sea life* on a chart tablet and draw a circle around it. Draw lines from the circle and write the children's ideas at the ends of those lines. Point out how much information the children know about the subject.

□ Discuss with the children how sharing is a pattern of your turn, my turn. Have the children play a partner game, such as jacks or cards, so the children experience the pattern in the game.

Books for Infants and Toddlers

Big Dog…Little Dog by P.D. Eastman

Goodnight Moon by Margaret Wise Brown

Opposites by Sandra Boynton

Books for Preschool Children

Brown Bear, Brown Bear, What Do You See? by Bill Martin, Jr.

Caps for Sale by Esphyr Slobodkina

The Doorbell Rang by Pat Hutchins

Epossumondas by Coleen Salley

Five Little Monkeys Jumping on the Bed by Eileen Christelow

Fortunately by Remy Charlip

Have You Seen My Duckling? by Nancy Tafuri

Jump, Frog, Jump by Robert Kalan

Rosie's Walk by Pat Hutchins

The Very Busy Spider by Eric Carle

The Very Hungry Caterpillar by Eric Carle

We're Going on a Bear Hunt by Michael Rosen

Books for School-Age Children

Calling Doctor Amelia Bedelia by Herman Parish

A Dog's Purpose by W. Bruce Cameron

Frog and Toad series by Arnold Lobel

Want to Read More?

Perry, B. 2000. How the brain learns best. *Instructor 6:* 34–37.

Sousa, D. 2005. *How the brain learns.* New York: Corwin Press.

Start Smart, Revised

Try, Try, Again

PRACTICE AND THE BRAIN

"Practice makes perfect," or does it? It is possible to repeat a skill over time and never improve. If we practice without knowing how to improve, no matter how much we practice, we will not improve. According to *How the Brain Learns* (Sousa, 2005), three things are necessary for practice to improve performance:

1. We need to understand the skill and how we will use it.
2. We must understand how to apply the skill to various situations.
3. We must be able to analyze our performance and be able to figure out how we can fine-tune to improve.

Practice improves a skill or helps us learn a concept only if we receive feedback from the environment. Repeating an activity or action over time increases recall. According to research, we have only a 10 percent chance of remembering something done once in 30 days, and a 90 percent chance of remembering something done six times in 30 days (Jensen, 2008).

IF WE PRACTICE WITHOUT KNOWING HOW TO IMPROVE,

...NO MATTER HOW MUCH WE PRACTICE, WE WILL NOT IMPROVE.

CHAPTER SEVENTEEN

Ideas to Build Brain Power with Practice

Experiences and Activities for Infants and Toddlers

☐ Set up an environment that encourages babies to practice newly learned skills. Pay attention to what the babies are practicing, and make sure they have opportunities to repeat those experiences.

☐ Know physical and cognitive developmental continuums. This way, when babies or toddlers master a new skill, it will be clear what comes next developmentally so you can support their attempts to master the next skill. The *Brigance Diagnostic Inventory of Early Development* published by Curriculum Associates is a viable source of skill sequence. Lists of scope and sequence of skills are also available on the following websites: www.childdevelopmentinfo.com/child-development/devsequence.shtml www.netdoctor.co.uk/health_advice/facts/baby_development_000607.htm

☐ Play games with little ones that allow them to practice skills such as tracking an item, rolling a ball, picking up small items, and so on.

Experiences and Activities for Preschool Children

☐ Become familiar with developmental learning continuums. Sometimes children will try to achieve a skill that is beyond their developmental abilities. For example, if a child is having trouble with detecting patterns, she may need more practice with classification. She needs to understand classification before she can learn notice patterns. Children who have trouble with rhyming words may need more experience exploring the concept of same and different. If you know the sequence in which skills develop, you are better prepared to offer feedback. (See website information above for information on developmental continuums. *Count on Math* and *Creating Readers*, which are both published by Gryphon House, provide continuum information and activities for math and literacy, respectively. Bonnie Campbell Hill has several reading and writing continuums and listening and speaking continuums (www.bonniecampbellhill.com/support.php).

☐ When introducing a skill, model it first. Offer the children information in small doses and gradually add more information as children show understanding. For example, when learning to create patterns, introduce horizontal patterns using two elements, such as buttons and crayons. Then move to more complex patterns by increasing the number of elements as well as the directions of the patterns.

INTRODUCE SIMPLE PATTERNS FIRST, AND THEN MOVE TO MORE COMPLEX PATTERNS.

Start Smart, Revised

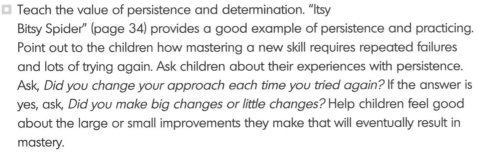

- Utilize peer teaching. It is often easier for children to provide clear feedback to each other than it is for adults to provide that feedback. Children speak the same language and share similar perspectives.

- Teach the value of persistence and determination. "Itsy Bitsy Spider" (page 34) provides a good example of persistence and practicing. Point out to the children how mastering a new skill requires repeated failures and lots of trying again. Ask children about their experiences with persistence. Ask, *Did you change your approach each time you tried again?* If the answer is yes, ask, *Did you make big changes or little changes?* Help children feel good about the large or small improvements they make that will eventually result in mastery.

- Offer feedback in a positive, helpful, and specific manner. Asking children to explain their work helps you know what they understand and, therefore, what specific feedback will be useful and supportive.

- Do not overload the children's daily schedule. Children do not have time to reflect on what they have done in a day if they are always busy with activities. Reflection is critical to improvement. Everyone needs time to reflect in order to evaluate and contemplate where they are and to decide what they need to become better at what they are doing.

- Offer children practice opportunities as soon as possible after introducing a skill. Provide frequent opportunities for children to repeat a skill so they become comfortable and proficient at it. Ask children to evaluate how they are doing and offer them your feedback. Experience wires the brain. Repetition strengthens the wiring.

Experiences and Activities for School-Age Children

- Create opportunities for school-age children to teach younger children. Peer teaching is a great tool for both parties. It lets young children receive information or learn about new skills in simple ways the children can understand. Peer teaching also helps school-age children develop patience, commitment, and determination.

- Encourage the children to think of skills or information they learned fairly quickly and proficiently. How did they learn these skills? Was the information provided to them in small, limited segments? Did the children receive feedback during the learning process? Did the children self-evaluate the learning process?

Ideas to Use with Two or More Children

- Discuss persistence as it relates to group activities such as putting on a play or playing a game of baseball. What happens if someone refuses to practice? How does one person's failure to practice impact the whole project?
- Place a puzzle with many pieces on a table, and designate the puzzle as a group project. Discuss progress each day.
- Invite children to create "persistence" mottos that they will all use for reminding each other to stick with a task. Encourage children to support each other's efforts by using the mottos.

Books for Infants and Toddlers

How Do Dinosaurs Clean their Rooms? by Jane Yolen
I Am 3! Look What I Can Do by Maria Carluccio

Books for Preschool Children

Itsy Bitsy Spider by Iza Trapani
Max Found Two Sticks by Brian Pinkney
Whistle for Willie by Ezra Jack Keats

Books for School-Age Children

I Spy Treasure Hunt by Jean Marzollo
When I Was Five by Arthur Howard

Want to Read More?

Jensen. E. 2008. *Brain-based learning: The new paradigm of teaching.* New York: Corwin Press

Shenk, D. 2010. *The genius in all of us: Why everything you've been told about genetics, talent, and IQ is wrong.* New York: Doubleday.

Sousa, D. 2005. *How the brain learns.* New York: Corwin Press.

CHAPTER EIGHTEEN

Solving Problems

PROBLEM SOLVING AND THE BRAIN

Problem solving is one of the brain's favorite exercises. Eric Jensen (2008) says that solving challenging problems is the single best way to "grow" a better brain. Problem solving causes synapses to form, chemicals to activate, and blood flow to increase in the brain. The brain learns when it is confronted with a problem (Jensen, 2008). When the brain encounters only routine situations or previously processed information, the brain simply repeats patterns and programs it has already learned. This is called *replication of habit* and, according to researchers, too much of it will interfere with new learning (Jensen, 2008). Problems force the brain to reconfigure its programs and patterns and, in doing so, the possibility for new learning emerges.

Supporting the notion that problems create the opportunity for new learning, researchers state that when a learner is in suspense, surprise, or uncertainty, the learner can develop a richer understanding of content (Jensen, 2008). See the chapter on novelty, pages 89–93.

> PROBLEM SOLVING CAUSES SYNAPSES TO FORM, CHEMICALS TO ACTIVATE,

> AND BLOOD FLOW TO INCREASE IN THE BRAIN.

Children's brains grow and develop at an amazing rate. Children as young as 12 months old are beginning to start simple problem-solving activities, such as using a chair to pull up or pulling a blanket to retrieve a toy on top of it. Between the ages of four and seven, the right hemispheres of children's brains are busy forging connections, a process that is strengthened by concrete problem-solving experiences. Between the ages of 9 and 12, the left hemisphere of children's brains has a growth spurt, another development that is strengthened by problem-solving activities. By age 11, children are ready to explore complex abstractions and are using problem-solving skills on a regular basis (Hanaford, 2007).

Another benefit of problem solving is that it naturally fuels self-confidence. Think about the pleasure that comes from solving a problem. The successful solution of one problem fosters a positive attitude about the next challenge. The more adept children become at solving problems, the more successes they have under their belts, the more confident they are moving forward.

Ideas to Enhance Learning and Build Confidence with Problem Solving

Experiences and Activities for Infants and Toddlers

- As infants explore the relationship between cause and effect, they build the foundation for problem solving. Successful problem solving requires understanding the cause-and-effect relationship between the problem and the various solutions. Provide different cause-and-effect toys, experiences, and activities for infants. Even before a baby can understand your words, describe the cause-and-effect relationships that you see. Continue calling attention to these relationships as the children expand what they understand.
- The world presents toddlers with many problems to solve. For example, how to reach a ball that is under the feeding table, or how to stack blocks without having them fall.
  - Ask toddlers questions that require them to think of new ways to do things. For example, ask, *How can you make the sound of the rattle louder? How can you make it softer? How can you fill the bucket with blocks without touching them with your hands?*

EXPLORING CAUSE AND EFFECT IS THE FOUNDATION FOR PROBLEM SOLVING.

Start Smart, Revised

Experiences and Activities for Preschool Children

- Teach the process of problem solving. This process must be learned, and the children will need guidance. Discuss each step of the problem-solving process as children apply it. After a few experiences, the process should become automatic.

Step 1	Identify and articulate the problem.
Step 2	Brainstorm possible solutions.
Step 3	Evaluate possible solutions in terms of resources required.
Step 4	Select one of the solutions.
Step 5	Try it out.
Step 6	Evaluate the results. If the first choice of solutions does not work, go back to Step 3 and try again.

When child-sized problems occur, let children solve them. Do not solve problems for the children; help them through the process. For example, if some juice spills, let the children experiment with different options for cleaning it up (sponge, dishcloth, napkin). Fortunately, it does not matter to the brain if the problem solving is successful. At this stage of brain development, it is the process that counts (Jensen, 2008).

PROBLEM SOLVING NATURALLY FUELS SELF-CONFIDENCE.

- Problem solving generally means coming up with new or different ideas. Make sure children have plenty of different experiences. For example, ask the children how they might change the end of a story and how their new ending alters the story. Ask the children how they might create a paintbrush if they had no brushes to use. Challenge the children to think of ways to move across the playground other than walking.

- Read stories that focus on problem solving, such as *Stone Soup* by Marcia Brown, *Swimmy* by Leo Lionni, *The Three Billy Goats Gruff* by Paul Galdone, *Moira's Birthday* by Robert Munsch, and *Fish Out of Water* by Helen Palmer. Encourage the children to evaluate the solutions in each story. Ask, *How else might the problem have been solved?* Also read stories that present problems. Stop after the problem has been identified, and invite children to brainstorm solutions. *The Doorbell Rang* by Pat Hutchins is a good example of this type of story.

- Use a story, such as *Imogene's Antlers* by David Small, as a springboard to encourage children to write or dictate their own problem-and-solution stories. In *Imogene's Antlers,* Imogene wakes up with antlers on her head and spends the day solving the problems that come with having a pair of antlers on one's head. At the end of the story, the antlers disappear but a new problem arises—a peacock tail. Children can use the story ending as a spark to begin their own stories. *David's Father* by Robert Munsch is another good story to jump-start this activity.

- Children use a variety of skills when they solve problems. Children need to know how to evaluate, synthesize, and analyze a situation or problem, and how to apply what they know to a situation. Ask the children questions that encourage them to use higher-level thinking skills. For example, the following are some questions you might ask after reading *The Three Billy Goats Gruff.*

  - **Evaluation:** Do you think it was okay for the small billy goat and the medium-size billy goat to tell the troll to wait for their bigger brother? Why or why not?
  - **Synthesis:** How would the story be different if the troll were friendly?
  - **Application:** The troll used his ugly face to scare the goats. Can you think of other ways the troll could have frightened the goats?
  - **Analysis:** Which part of the story could happen in real life? Which parts are make-believe?

> COMPARING AND CONTRASTING PROVIDE PRACTICE IN SCRUTINIZING POSSIBLE SOLUTIONS TO PROBLEMS.

- Provide opportunities for children to compare and contrast stories, activities, games, and concepts. Comparing and contrasting provide practice in scrutinizing possible solutions to problems. Try comparing two versions of *The Little Red Hen,* or ask questions such as *How is a bird different from a cat?*

COWS	COWS & HORSES	HORSES
walk and run	animals	walk and run
we drink their milk	have four legs	we don't drink their milk
moo	may live on farms	we can ride them
eat grass		neigh
		eat oats

▢ Use Venn diagrams to compare two items. For example, use a Venn diagram to compare how horses and cows are alike and how are they different.

▢ Ask the children "what if" questions. *What if red were the only color? What if children were in charge of parents? What if horses could ride people? What if dogs could talk?*

▢ Ask questions that require the children to exercise judgment. Ask, *Do you think all these marbles will fit in this jar?* or *Do you think it was all right for the Little Red Hen to refuse to share her bread?*

▢ Set up activities that require the children to engage in different kinds of problem solving. A few suggestions include:

  ▪ Mix one cup beans, one cup salt, and one cup rice together in a bowl. Provide the children with a strainer and a colander and tell them to separate the items in the bowl into three separate bowls—one with beans, one with salt, and one with rice. After the children are successful, ask them if they can think of any other way to accomplish the task.

  ▪ Place two long strips of masking tape on the floor, five feet apart. Ask the children how they could move a Ping Pong ball from one line to the other without touching it. (Some possibilities include blowing on the ball through a straw, fanning it with a magazine or book, blowing on it directly, or blowing on it through a paper towel tube.)

  ▪ Cut three or four sets of cat footprints and bird tracks from black construction paper. Tape the footprints on the floor with the line of bird prints perpendicular to the line of cat prints. The two sets of prints should meet at a right angle with only the cat prints continuing. Encourage the children to share their ideas of what happened. Children will guess things like the bird flew away, the cat ate the bird, and the bird hopped on the cat's back. Ask the children if there is any way they can know for sure what happened.

■ Fill a clear plastic cup with pebbles and then ask the children if the cup is full. If they say no, have the children add pebbles until everyone agrees that the cup is full. Then ask the children if they think anything else will fit into the cup. The children will probably say no. Pour either salt or sand into the cup. The children will be surprised to see that the cup will hold more. Point out how sand or salt fills in the spaces left between the pebbles. Ask the children if the cup is full now; the children will probably say yes. Pour water into the cup, showing how the cup can hold still more. The children will be surprised. Ask the children to think about why the cup could hold the water. Engage the children in a discussion about the different ways to think about the concept of *full*.

■ Give the children two coffee cans and several smaller items to place inside the cans (a roll of tape, a small book, a crayon, a block). Have the children place one item in each can and then roll the cans. Ask the children to explore and notice how the items inside the cans affect the way the cans roll. If the children want to race their cans, use masking tape as the finish line.

■ Model problem solving for the children. When it is appropriate, talk through different problems and the decision-making process you followed to find a solution.

☐ When children ask "why" questions, encourage them to think through the possible answers to their questions. For example, if a flashlight burns out, help the children come to the conclusion that the flashlight might need new batteries, instead of saying, "It probably needs new batteries."

☐ Teach the children riddles and introduce brainteasers. These can be great field trip activities. For example, while traveling to a field trip location, challenge the children to try to find things that are a certain color. When children get older, challenge them to find items with names that start with each letter of the alphabet.

☐ Read the children chapter books that use a problem-and-resolution format such as *Nate the Great* by Marjorie Weinman Sharmat and the *Frog and Toad* series by Arnold Lobel. Read one chapter each day and then engage the children in a discussion about the problem or plot as it unfolds.

PROBLEM-SOLVING IS ONE OF THE BRAIN'S FAVORITE EXERCISES.

Start Smart, Revised

◻ Use guidance strategies that include children's ideas and solutions. This encourages the children to think through problems and to be involved in the process of coming up with solutions to issues that arise in the classroom. This type of discussion and use of natural or logical consequences is far more beneficial to children's development of self-control than punishment handed down by adults. The following is one suggestion:

Crystal
Problem:
Four-year-old Crystal breaks the crayons in the art center after being reminded that broken crayons are difficult for other children to use.
Action:
Have a discussion with Crystal. Ask her for a solution. If she doesn't come up with one, give her three options.
Options:
1. Crystal can be prohibited from working in the art center for a specified period of time.
2. Crystal can try working with the crayons again to prove that she can use them without breaking them.
3. Crystal can choose a "crayon buddy" to work with her in the art center for the next week to help her remember that other children do not enjoy using broken crayons.

When the children are involved in choosing solutions to problems and have a bit of control over the situation, it increases the likelihood that the children will follow through on the decision. However, if Crystal cannot choose, choose for her.

◻ Help the children recycle or reuse paper and other materials used in the classroom. Explain that this is an individual solution to a global problem.

Experiences and Activities for School-Age Children

◻ Read chapter books that use a problem-and-solution format, such as *Nancy Drew* and *The Hardy Boys*. Read one chapter each day and talk with the children about the story's problem or plot as it unfolds.

◻ Pose larger problems to the children and challenge them to suggest solutions. For example, *How can we get people to pick up litter in the park? How can we get more people to attend the school play? How can we raise money for a field trip? How can we campaign against (or for) year-round school? What rules can we put in place regarding the proper care of outdoor equipment?*

◻ Science experiments and projects are usually filled with problem-solving opportunities. Here are a few websites that provide simple science experiments and projects:

www.sciencemadesimple.com/projects.html

www.easy-kids-science-experiments.com/science-experiments-elementary.html

www.cool-scienceprojects.com/elementaryScienceProjects.html

Ideas to Use with Two or More Children

◻ Set up problem-focused scenarios and encourage the children to come up with solutions. For example, Lisa and Michael are playing with Michael's new trucks. When Heather shows up to play, there are three children but only two trucks. How many ways can the children think of to involve Heather in the play (share the trucks, let Heather work the service station or loading dock, put the trucks away and play with something else)?

◻ Help the children create puppet shows based on a problem. Let the children suggest various solutions and then act them out.

Books for Infants and Toddlers

Baby Faces by Margaret Miller

Where Is My Baby? by Harriet Ziefert

Where Is My Friend? by Simms Taback

SCIENCE EXPERIMENTS AND PROJECTS ARE USUALLY FILLED WITH PROBLEM-SOLVING OPPORTUNITIES.

Where Is My House? by Simms Taback

Who Said Moo? by Harriet Ziefert

Books for Preschool Children

David's Father by Robert Munsch

The Doorbell Rang by Pat Hutchins

Imogene's Antlers by David Small

The Little Red Hen by Paul Galdone

Mike Mulligan and His Steam Shovel by Virginia Lee Burton

Moira's Birthday by Robert Munsch

Stone Soup by Marcia Brown

Swimmy by Leo Lionni

Three Billy Goats Gruff by Paul Galdone

Books for School-Age Children

Henry and Mudge and the Tall Tree House by Cynthia Rylant

Nate the Great series by Marjorie Weinman Sharmat

Want to Read More?

Carey, B. 2010. *Tracing the spark of creative problem-solving. New York Times,* December 7, D-2, New York edition.

Hannaford, C. 2007. *Smart moves: Why learning is not all in your head,* revised. Salt Lake City, UT: Great Rivers Publications.

Jensen, E. 2008. *Brain-based learning: The new paradigm of teaching.* New York: Corwin Press.

Mednick, S. 2009. Let me sleep on it: Creative problem solving enhanced by REM sleep. *Science Daily.* University of California: San Diego, CA.

Start Smart, Revised

Praise or Encouragement

REWARDS, PRAISE, AND THE BRAIN

Rewards are often used to motivate children to behave in a certain way. Generally, rewards do encourage predictable behavior. However, reward systems, if used too long and too frequently, can diminish the intrinsic joy children should feel as the motivation for learning. Children who receive bribes to complete work or for good behavior soon tire of the designated reward and begin to require a bigger and better reward. They learn to "work the system" rather than work or learn for the intrinsic satisfaction of such accomplishments. Some studies even suggest that excessive praise can cause children to develop performance anxiety. In one study, students who were praised prior to taking a skills test performed worse than students were not praised. Research suggests that "extrinsic motivation inhibits intrinsic motivation" (Jensen, 2008). Reward systems prevent children from establishing intrinsic motivation because there is rarely an incentive to be creative—only to perform or behave in the requested manner.

Using phrases such as "Good job!" and "Way to go!" is conditional feedback. It is based on the judgments and desires of the person delivering the praise. Praise teaches children how to manipulate their environment to receive external validation. Praise diminishes the sense of personal satisfaction a child might feel when completing a task (Kohn, 2005). Praise creates "praise junkies" and "people pleasers."

Encouragement, in contrast to praise, acknowledges what a child has accomplished. Encouragement reflects an appreciation of the effort regardless of the task completion or behavior. Encouragement also supports a child's self-evaluation.

Children need a balance. A little praise can motivate. Constant praise inhibits children's motivation. Encouragement is by far a better teaching tool. It provides useful information to the learner.

Ideas to Build Motivation with Encouragement

Experiences and Activities for Infants and Toddlers
- "I love you" and a hug are all the encouragement an infant needs.
- Use encouraging statements with toddlers. See the chart in this chapter for suggestions.

Experiences and Activities for Preschool Children
- Reduce the amount of praise you use with children. Replace it with feedback and encouraging statements. Here are a few examples:

Praising Statement	Encouraging Statement
"That's a great painting, Tiffany."	The red and yellow colors you used for the trees creates a fall look.
"Good job coming down the slide."	"You came down the slide feet first and landed right in my arms."
"Good job on the puzzle"	"You finished the entire puzzle. That took determination."
"High five for your drawing!"	"I can tell you put a lot of effort into your drawing, Evan."
"I am so proud of you."	"You seem to enjoy math."

ENCOURAGEMENT REFLECTS AN APPRECIATION OF EFFORT REGARDLESS OF THE TASK COMPLETION OR BEHAVIOR

- Help the children learn to evaluate their own efforts. Let them critique themselves.
- Focus on process as opposed to product. For example, instead of saying, *Your building turned out great, Ginny,* say, *Gee, Ginny, that building shows a lot of hard work that you did all by yourself.*
- Set children up for success. For example, saying, *Gabrielle, you are always so nice,* sets her up for failure because no one is nice all the time. Keep statements specific to individual children and to children's immediate accomplishment. *Gabrielle, helping Quinn zip his coat was thoughtful.*
- Use a natural voice when offering support to children. Be specific and sincere.
- Allow children to have choices. Choices increase intrinsic motivation. Giving children choices increases the possibility that they will accept the chosen idea.
- Encourage children's progress by making accurate statements of improvement. For example, *Steve, you set the table with all the silverware today.*

- Support the processes children use instead of only commenting on the finished products. For example, say, *I noticed you spent a lot of time looking for just the right colors for your picture, Rosie,* instead of *Rosie, your picture looks terrific.* Encouraging effort helps children focus on the most meaningful part of the activity and encourages the transfer of effort to the next task.
- Avoid promising concrete rewards for appropriate behaviors. Instead, help children feel content with their appropriate behaviors. Remember, children earn and lose privileges. All people are entitled to food, shelter, safety, and education. Everything else is a privilege that can be earned or lost when behavior warrants. For example, José can earn the privilege of playing in the block center. He can lose this privilege if he breaks the center rules.

- Children with special needs will be more dependent on rewards. It is acceptable to use rewards with children who need an immediate reinforcement for their accomplishments. It is advisable, however, to try to balance praise and reward statements with children who have special needs.

Experiences and Activities for School-Age Children
- Invite children to help you think of encouraging statements to replace the typical statement of praise, such as *Good job, Terrific*, and *Way to go!*
- Avoid comparisons and competitions. Saying, *I like the way Linda is sitting*, puts Linda in competition with her friends. It also demoralizes others who were sitting quietly but were not recognized. Instead, say, *Oh, my, we have forgotten how to sit in our circle! Who can show me how we should sit?"*

Books for Infants and Toddlers

Goodnight, Baby Bear by Frank Asch   *No, No, Yes, Yes* by Leslie Patricelli
Just Like Daddy by Frank Asch

Books for Preschool Children

Amazing Grace by Mary Hoffman   *The Little Red Hen* by Paul Galdone
Dance, Tanya by Patricia Lee Gauch   *Whistle for Willie* by Ezra Jack Keats
I Can Share by Karen Katz

Books for School-Age Children

Emma's Strange Pet by Jean Little
Ramona Quimby, Age 8 by Beverly Cleary

Want to Read More?

Amabile, T. 1992. *Growing up creative: Nurturing a lifetime of creativity*, 2nd edition. Amherst, ME. Creative Education Foundation.

Jensen, E. 2008. *Brain-based learning: The new paradigm of teaching.* New York: Corwin Press.

Kohn, A. 1999. *Punished by rewards: The trouble with gold stars, incentive plans, A's, praise, and other bribes.* New York: Mariner Books.

Kohn, A. 2000. Hooked on praise. *Parents Magazine.*

Kohn, A. 2001. Five reasons to stop saying "Good Job!" *Young Children* 56 (5): 24–28. Washington, DC: NAEYC.

Spanish, Japanese, Vietnamese

CHAPTER TWENTY

SECOND-LANGUAGE LEARNING AND THE BRAIN

> THE BRAIN ASSIGNS A NEURON TO EVERY SOUND IN A CHILD'S NATIVE LANGUAGE.

Between the fourth and eighth months of life, the brain assigns a neuron to every sound in a child's native language. The neurons are connected and strengthened as the child begins to connect sounds and speech. If more than one language is heard, the brain assigns neurons to the second language as well (Bortfeld, Wruck, Boas, 2007; Friederici, Fredrich, & Christophe, 2007).

During the early years, a child's brain is highly receptive to language. Researchers propose that exposing children to other languages helps them build neural networks that will make it easier to learn other languages later (Kovelman, Baker, & Petitto, 2008; Kovelman, Shalinsky et al., 2008).

Positron-emission tomography (PET) scans show that when children grow up learning two languages, the brain uses a single area to store all the language activity. PET scans of people who learn a second language at a later age show that the brain stores the two languages in separate areas (Bloch et al., 2009; Hernandez & Li, 2007).

Listening to language from a secondary source, such as the television or a CD, can support language development, but children need human interaction to effectively learn to speak both their native language and a second language.

Research indicates that the brain's affinity for language remains active up to about the age of 10, so the appropriate time for formal instruction is between 6 and 10. If taught a language in this time frame, the result should be a child who speaks a second language without accent, and without having to mentally translate from one language to the other. After age 10, a child can certainly still learn a second language, but the task will become increasingly difficult and it is unlikely that the child will speak the second language fluently or without mentally translating the two languages (Sousa, 2011).

Scholars have long debated whether language constrains the ways we think. Now, neuroscientists studying reading disorders are beginning to consider the possibility that the actual character of the text itself may help to shape the brain. Recent neurological studies (Hotz, 2008) reveal that different languages are stored in different places in the brain. For example, children who learn to read and write Chinese use different parts of their brains than children who learn to read and write English (Hotz, 2008).

* Additional research on page 172 in the Appendix.

Ideas to Build Brain Power with a Second Language

Experiences and Activities for Infants and Toddlers

☐ If possible, talk to babies and toddlers in a second language every day. Repeat the same vocabulary words to the children throughout the day. Use phrases like *good morning* and *goodbye*. Refer to the children's family members using words from a second language. Here are names for family member names in four languages:

English	Spanish	Japanese	Vietnamese
mother	mamá	haha	me
father	papá	chichi	cha
brother	hijo	otouto	em trai
sister	hija	ane em	em gái
baby	bebé	akachan	em bé
family	la familia	kazoku	gia-dình

☐ Sing familiar songs in other languages. Here is "Good Morning to You" in four languages.

Good Morning to You (English)
Good morning to you,
Good morning to you,
I greet you in English—
Good morning to you.

Bonjour Mesdames (French)
Bonjour Mesdames,
Bonjour Messieurs,
I greet you in French—
Bonjour mesdames,
bonjour messieurs.

Buenos días (Spanish)
¡Buenos días a ti!
¡Buenos días a ti!
I greet you in Spanish
¡Buenos días a ti!

Guten Morgen (German)
Guten morgen, du.
Guten morgen, du.
I greet you in German
Guten morgen, du.

- Invite family members who speak other languages to volunteer during tummy time or play time.
- Play games with toddlers using words from a second language. Following are translations of *peekaboo* in Spanish (*cucu*), Japanese (*inai inai, ba!*), and Vietnamese (*tù My,nghĩa Mỹ*). Here is "I'm gonna get you!" in Spanish: *Ite voy a agarrar!*.

Here are two surprise games in English and Spanish:

'Round the House

'Round the house, (Circle index finger on baby's hand.)
'Round the house,
Goes the little mousie.
Up the stairs, (Slowly "walk" fingers up baby's arm.)
Up the stairs
In the little housie. (Tickle baby's neck gently)

Vueltas y más vueltas adapted by Emilia Rivas

Vueltas y más vueltas, (Circle index finger on baby's hand.)
vueltas muchas vueltas,
da este ratoncito.
La escalera sube, ("Walk" fingers up baby's arm.)
sube, sube y sube,
¡buscando a un bebito! (Point to baby's tummy.)

Little Snail

Slowly, slowly creeps the garden snail
(Creep fingers up baby's arm.)
Up, up, up the winding trail.
Quickly, quickly, bumblebees swarm
("Fly" fingers around baby.)
Here and there and under
your arm. (Tickle baby
gently under the arm.)

THE BRAIN'S AFFINITY FOR LANGUAGE REMAINS ACTIVE UP TO ABOUT THE AGE OF 10.

El caracolito adapted by Emilia Rivas

Sube despacito, el caracolito (Creep fingers slowly up baby's arm.)
sube dando vueltas por el caminito.
Viene por aquí, se va para allá (Move fingers around.)
y bajo tu brazo él se esconderá. (Tickle baby gently under the arm.)

Experiences and Activities for Preschool Children

☐ If you speak a second language, take 10–20 minutes a day to intentionally teach children this language.

☐ Teach simple words in another language. For example, *agua* for "water," *adios* for "goodbye," and *bonjour* for "good morning." Here are the numbers 1–10 in four languages:

Spanish	1. *uno*, 2. *dos*, 3. *tres*, 4. *cuatro*, 5. *cinco*, 6. *seis*, 7. *siete*, 8. *ocho*, 9. *nueve*, 10. *diez.* For pronunciation visit: www.enchantedlearning.com/language/spanish/numbers/10s.shtml
Japanese	1. ichi, 2. *ni*, 3. *san*, 4. *shi*, 5. *go*, 6. *roku*, 7. *shichi*, 8. *hachi*, 9. *kyuu*, 10. *juu* For pronunciation visit: www.learnjapanesewordsandphrases.com/learnjapanesenumbers.html
Chinese	1. *yi*, 2. *erh*, 3. *san*, 4. *ss*, 5. *wu*, 6. *lio*, 7. *ba*, 8. *chi*, 9. *jio*, 10. *shyr* For pronunciation visit: www.chinese-word.com/numbers_1_100/html/index.html
French	1. *un*, 2. *deux*, 3. *trois*, 4. *quatre*, 5. *cinq*, 6. *six*, 7. *sept*, 8. *huit*, 9. *neuf*, 10. *dix* For pronunciation visit: french.about.com/od/vocabulary/ss/numbers.htm

☐ Solicit help from someone who speaks another language, perhaps a senior citizen or a high school student.

☐ Sing songs with lyrics in foreign languages, such as "Frére Jacques," or sing translation of popular children's songs, such as "Good Morning to You" (see page 135) and "Itsy Bitsy Spider" (translated below in Spanish).

La araña chiquitita by Emilia Rivas

La araña chiquitita subió, subió y subió,
vino la lluvia y al suelo la arrastró,
el Sol salió de nuevo y todo lo secó,"
Y la araña chiquitita subió, subió y subió.

☐ Encourage children to play with peers who speak another language.

Activities and Experiences for School-Age Children

- ☐ Help children find a pen pal from another country. Encourage the children to write to their pen pals using their native languages and then attempt to translate to their pen pals' native languages.
- ☐ Teach children American Sign Language, which is a second language. Invite a sign-language interpreter to visit your class.

agua

bonjour

adios

Ideas to Use with Two or More Children

- ☐ If there is a bilingual child in the class, ask that child to help teach the rest of the class words in his or her second language.
- ☐ Arrange times when the children in your class can meet and talk to children who speak a second language. For example, schedule a joint field trip with a bilingual school.

Books for Infants and Toddlers

Caritas by Todd Parr
¡Cucu! by Roberta Grobel Intrater
Dulces Suenos: Sleep! by Roberta Grobel Intrater

Books for Preschool Children

Abuela by Arthur Dorros
Bread Is for Eating by David and Phyllis Gershator
A Chance for Esperanza by Pam Schiller
Emeka's Gift by Ifeoma Onyefulu
Madeleine by Ludwig Bemelmans
The Park Bench by Fumiko Takeshita

IF LEARNED LATER IN LIFE, DIFFERENT LANGUAGES ARE STORED IN DIFFERENT PLACES IN THE BRAIN.

Books for School-Age Children

If America Were a Village: A Book about the People of the United States by David J. Smith

This Tree Is Older Than You Are by Naomi Shihab Nye

Want to Read More?

Asher, J. J. 2000. *Learning another language through actions,* 6th edition. Los Gatos, CA: Sky Oaks Productions.

Bortfield, H., Wruck, E. & Boas, D.A. 2007. Assessing infants' cortical response to speech using near-infared spectroscopy. *Neuroimage* 34: 407–415.

Bloch, C., Kaiser, A., Kuenzli, E., Zappatore, D., Haller, S., & Franceschini, R., 2009. The age of second language acquisition determines the variablility in activation elicited by narration in three languages in Broca's and Wernicke's area. *Neuropsychologia* 47: 625–633.

Friederici, A. D., Friedrich, M., & Christophe, A. 2007. Brain responses in 4-month-old infants are already language specific. *Current Biology,* 17 (14): 1208-1211.

Gabriele, J., Hedden, T., Ketay, S., & Aron, A. 2008, January. Culture influences brain function. Psychological Science. Washington, DC: Association for Psychological Sciences.

Hernandez, A. E. & Li, P. 2007. Age of acquisition: Its neural and computational mechanisms. *Psychological Bulletin,* 133: 638–650.

Hotz, R. L. 2008. How the brain learns to read can depend on the language. *Wall Street Journal,* May 2, *Science Journal.* A10.

Kovelman, I., Baker, S.A., & Petitto, L.A. 2008, January. Bilingual and monolingual brains compared: A functional magnetic resonance imaging investigation of syntactic processing and a possible "neural signature" of bilingualism. *Journal of Cognitive Neuroscience,* 20 (1): 153-169.

Kovelman, I., Shalinsky, M.H., Berens, M.S, & Petitto, L.A. 2008. Shining new light on the brain's "Bilingual Signature," A functional near infrared spectroscopy investigation of semantic processing. *Neuroimage,* 39 (3): 1457-1471.

Siok, W. T., Spinks, J. A., Jin Zhen, T., & Li, H. 2009. Developmental dyslexia is characterized by the co-existence of visuospatial and phonological disorders in Chinese children. *Current Biology* 19 (19): 890–892.

Sousa, D. 2011. *How the ELL brain learns.* New York: Corwin Press.

Start Smart, Revised

What Does It Mean?

SENSE, MEANING, AND THE BRAIN

Getting information transferred to long-term memory is critical because the brain cannot use what it has not stored. For the brain to store information in its long-term memory, the information must meet two criteria. First, the information must make sense, and, second, it must have meaning. (See the chapter on patterns, pages 107–113.)

Sense means that the brain can fit the information into existing understanding. *Meaning* means the brain regards the information as relevant. It is possible for something to make sense but be of little relevance. Meaning is a way of establishing relevance. In determining what information makes it into the brain's long-term memory, both meaning and sense are significant. Many things make sense to us (movies we watch, books we read, conversations we have, things we see at the park), but the brain does not store that information in long-term memory if it does not seem relevant to us. Have you ever gone to a movie and not been able to remember the plot a few weeks later? If the movie has meaning because it is a movie about teachers and you are a teacher, you have a far greater chance of remembering not only the plot, but specific details as well (Sousa, 2005).

> BOTH MEANING AND SENSE ARE IMPORTANT.

Teachers generally spend most of their teaching time and planning time figuring out how to help children make sense of information. Some researchers believe that meaning is more likely than sense to increase the possibility that the brain will retain learning. With this in mind, it is important to explore ways to make learning relevant (Sousa, 2005).

Ideas to Increase Memory with Sense and Meaning

Experiences and Activities for Infants and Toddlers

- Little ones understand our words and tone long before we may think they do. Talk to babies about how they will use the new skills they are learning. For example, when a toddler is learning to control a fork, encourage his effort by using encouraging words and tone. For example, say, *Soon you will be feeding yourself without spilling any food on your tray.* When a baby is starting to crawl, say, *You will be going anywhere you want before long.*
- Introduce a new toy or game by pointing out how the new item is similar to a toy or game that is familiar to the child. Say, *This game is like the one you play with the frog. You push the buttons to hear the sounds.*
- When it is necessary to say no to something a child wants, be sure to state the reason why. *We cannot stay outside any longer. It is time for lunch.*

Experiences and Activities for Preschool Children

- Ask questions that encourage children to match new information to their experiences. For example, after reading *The Three Billy Goats Gruff,* ask if the children can think of a time when they were frightened like the small and medium-sized goats were. Or, ask the children which character in the story they would like to be and why. This kind of questioning helps children connect a story to their own lives, making the story meaningful and relevant.
- Ask questions that help children recall the sequence of the story—the beginning, middle, and end.
- Invite children to think of ways they will apply what they are learning. Listen to the children's answers and write them down on chart paper. For example, if the children are learning about one-to-one correspondence, they might realize they can use this skill to pass out supplies or set the table for snack.

- When teaching content or skills, present the whole—the big picture—before focusing on specific parts. It is common to start with the parts and build to the whole. Sense and meaning are easier to achieve if children see the big picture first. For example, when practicing letter recognition and sounds with the children, start by pointing out words in written text, and then point out the letters within the words. Invite children to write their names on 6" x 4" pieces of poster board. Next, set out child-safe scissors and have the children cut between the letters of their names, making name puzzles. Working these self-made puzzles allows children to see the sense and meaning in the part-to-whole relationship of letters and words.

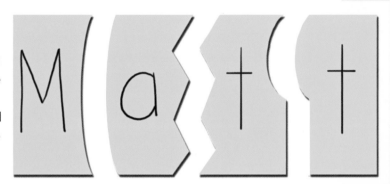

- Follow the children's interests by listening to the questions they ask and observing the choices they make. Children (and adults) are more motivated to understand (make sense of) things in which they have an interest.

- Offer experiences in meaningful context. It is easier for children to understand the importance of good manners when they learn about manners while playing and interacting with other children. Learning about manners abstractly separates the lesson from its context, its meaning.

- Make home-school connections. For example, if children are learning about insects at school, suggest that they help their parents make gardens at home. If the children are learning about matching at school, suggest that parents let their children help put the groceries away or match and fold clean socks. The children will have fun applying their ability to match like items in a meaningful context.

- Ask the children reflective questions, such as *What will you do with what you have learned?* For example, if Sage just hit Steve, ask Sage how he will handle the situation next time. This helps children make sense of the situation, understand the relevance of their experience, and, therefore, remember it. According to research, we remember 20 percent of what we read, 30 percent of what we hear, 50 percent of what we read and hear, 70 percent of what we say, and 90 percent of what we say and do (Sousa, 2005).

Experiences and Activities for School-Age Children

- ☐ Make sure children understand how they will be able to apply the information they learn. For example, tell the children that when they learn to read they will be able to lead a book read-along in the classroom. Introduce content in ways so that children will understand why it is important. For example, tell the children a story about a child who is able to use newly acquired reading skills.
- ☐ When the children answer a question incorrectly, give them the question to which their answer applies. For example, *That is the correct answer if I had asked* _____ .
- ☐ Encourage older children to help younger ones. Often older children are better than adults at offering younger children the right words to help establish sense and meaning.

Books for Infants and Toddlers

The Baby Dances by Kathy Henderson
Dance Me, Daddy by Cindy Morgan

Books for Preschool Children

Apples and Pumpkins by Anne Rockwell
Here Are My Hands by Bill Martin Jr.
The Holes in Your Nose by Genichiro Yagyu
The Kissing Hand by Audrey Penn
Leo the Late Bloomer by Robert Kraus
Something Special by Nicola Moon

Books for School-Age Children

Amos and Boris by William Steig
You Read to Me, I'll Read to You by Mary Ann Hoberman

Want to Read More?

Jonassen, D.H. & Land S.M. 2000. *Theoretical foundations of learning environments.* Mahwah, NJ: Lawrence Erlbaum Associates.
Sousa, D. 2005. *How the brain learns,* revised. New York: Corwin Press.

The Hand-Brain Connection

SMALL MUSCLES AND THE BRAIN

> THE BRAIN AND THE BODY ARE A COORDINATED UNIT.

When children (and adults) use their fingers, this action not only stimulates their muscles, it also stimulates their brains. Studies have confirmed that physical activity stimulates the brain. The brain and the body are a coordinated unit. The brain supports all motor functions and works together with the body to try to execute any task that a body asks of it. Small-muscle activities are some of the first ways we forge connections in the brain. This means, essentially, that the body trains the brain—the brain directs movement, and that movement shapes the brain (Ratey & Hagerman, 2008).

Research has validated the positive effects of touching textured materials (tactile stimulation). In fact, researchers suggest that continued use of our fingers helps people stay mentally alert as they grow older. There has never been a concert pianist who had problems with senility (Jensen, 2008). The brain activates the hands and feet, and it appears that the reverse is also true (Jensen, 2008).

Based on research performed over the last 15 years, Dr. Derek Cabrera has concluded that hands-on explorations contribute not only to the understanding of abstract concepts but also to four critical-thinking skills essential to learning: making distinctions, recognizing relationships, organizing systems, and seeing things from multiple perspectives. This higher-level thinking starts with touch. The sense of touch helps children to ground abstract ideas in concrete experiences. Hip-hip hooray for early childhood professionals! We have held this theory as truth for a long time.

Ideas for Using Small Muscles to Stimulate Learning

Experiences and Activities for Infants and Toddlers

☐ Provide small toys for babies to pick up. **Safety Note:** Test all toys with a child safety choke tester to ensure that the toys do not pose a choking hazard.

☐ Play with baby's fingers and toes. Use finger and toe games such as This Little Piggy and Pat-a-Cake (see below).

Pat-a-Cake (Version 1)
Pat-a-cake, pat-a-cake, baker's man.
Bake me a cake as fast as you can;
Pat it and prick it and mark it with B,
Put it in the oven for baby and me.
(With older children, substitute their first initials and name for B and baby.)

Pat-a-Cake (Version 2)
Patty cake, patty cake, baker's man.
Bake me a cake as fast as you can;
Roll it up, roll it up;
And throw it in a pan!
Patty cake, patty cake, baker's man.

☐ Teach ASL signs to children. Infants are ready for sign language around eight months. *Simple Signing with Young Children* by Carol Garboden Murray is an excellent resource.

☐ Provide finger foods for children during snack and lunchtime.

SMALL-MUSCLE ACTIVITIES ARE SOME OF THE FIRST WAYS WE FORGE CONNECTIONS IN THE BRAIN.

Experiences and Activities for Preschool Children

☐ Perform fingerplays every day. Here are two examples:

Open, Shut Them

Open, shut them, open, shut them,
Give a little clap.
Open, shut them, open, shut them,
Put them in your lap.

Creep them, creep them, creep them,
creep them,
Right up to your chin.
Open wide your smiling mouth,
But do not let them in.

Creep them, creep them, creep them,
creep them,
Past your cheeks and chin,
Open wide your smiling eyes,
Peeking in—Boo!

Creep them, creep them, creep them,
creep them,
Right down to your toes.
Let them fly up in the air and
Bop you on the nose!

Open, shut them, open, shut them,
Give a little clap.
Open, shut them, open, shut them,
Put them in your lap.

Ten Little Fingers

I have ten little fingers,
And they all belong to me.
I can make them do things.
Would you like to see?

I can shut them up tight,
Or open them wide.
I can put them together,
Or make them all hide.
I can make them jump high,
Or make them go low.
I can fold them up quietly,
And sit just so.

- Encourage children to work puzzles, put together Tinker Toys, or use lacing boards and pegboards. Create homemade puzzles by cutting greeting cards or fronts of cereal boxes into puzzle pieces. Challenge older children to make their own puzzles.
- Play clapping games. Who Stole the Cookie from the Cookie Jar? or Miss Mary Mack are games preschoolers enjoy.

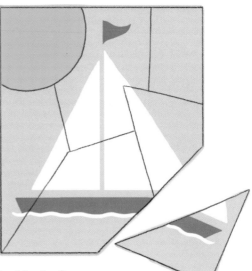

Who Stole the Cookie from the Cookie Jar?

Say this chant as you pat your thighs then snap in a rhythmic motion. Continue until everyone has been "accused" at least once.
Who stole the cookie from the cookie jar?
(Name) *stole the cookie from the cookie jar.*
Who, me?
Yes, you.
Couldn't be.
Then who?
(New name chosen by the first accused) *stole the cookie from the cookie jar.*
Who, me?
Yes, you.
Couldn't be.
Then who?

WHEN CHILDREN USE THEIR FINGERS, THIS ACTION NOT ONLY STIMULATES THEIR MUSCLES,

IT ALSO STIMULATES THEIR BRAINS.

Miss Mary Mack

This game requires two people. Pair two children or be the child's partner. Clap hands together and then against partner's hands; repeat.

Miss Mary Mack, Mack, Mack
All dressed in black, black, black,
With silver buttons, buttons, buttons
All down her back, back, back.
She asked her mother, mother, mother
For fifteen cents, cents, cents,
To see the elephants, elephants, elephants
Jump over the fence, fence, fence.
They jumped so high, high, high
They touched the sky, sky, sky.
And they never came down, down, down
'Til the Fourth of July, -ly, -ly,
And they never came down, down, down
'Til the Fourth of July.

- Bring the children on nature walks, and encourage them to collect small items. Turn a piece of masking tape so the sticky side is facing out. Wear it as a bracelet or belt. Help the child attach the collected items to the bracelet or belt.
- Encourage water-play activities that exercise the children's small muscles. Provide eyedroppers, sponges, or basters that the children can use to transfer water. Using a bar of soap in the water table is both a nice tactile activity as well as an opportunity to develop small muscles.
- Invite children to use tweezers or clothespins to pick up small items, such as buttons or seeds, and transfer these items from one container to another.
- Suggest that the children fingerpaint. Add sand or salt to the paints to encourage more exploration. Let the children explore fingerpainting with shaving cream to make snowy paintings.
- Provide paper and suggest that children to tear it into various shapes. Invite the children to glue their shapes to another piece of paper to create pictures.

■ Make Gak or Goop for the children to explore. They can squeeze, roll, pat, and create with it.

Gak (without Borax)
1 cup very warm water
food coloring
2 cups cornstarch
mixing bowl
mixing spoon
storage bag or container

Pour the warm (almost hot) water and food coloring into the bowl.
Stir until combined. Add the cornstarch a little at a time. Stir until smooth.
Add more cornstarch if the mixture is too runny; add more very warm water
if the mixture is too thick. Keep the mixture moist by storing
in a re-sealable bag or container.

Goop
2 cups salt
1 cup water, divided
1 cup cornstarch
measuring cups
saucepan
stove or hot plate

Cook salt and ½ cup of water for 4–5 minutes over medium-high heat, until the salt is
dissolved. Remove from heat. Add cornstarch and ½ cup water. Return to heat.
Stir until mixture thickens. Store in plastic bag or covered container.

■ Provide playdough, pipe cleaners, buttons, and cookie cutters for the children to explore. Using these materials will develop the children's finger muscles.

■ Provide children with a pastry brush, scoop, and sand. Invite them to use the brush to sweep the sand into the scoop and dump it into a container.

- Provide peas or peanuts for the children to shell. This works the small muscles in the children's hands. Make peanut butter or pea soup afterwards for the children to enjoy. **Safety note:** Check for allergies to peanuts before proceeding with this activity.
- Challenge the children to try eating with chopsticks. It can be a challenging (and fun) experience!
- Bake bread and have the children help knead the dough.
- Invite children to help prepare snacks and meals. They can break up lettuce, wash fruits and vegetables, cut up soft fruits with a plastic knife, and help measure ingredients. Cleaning up after snacks and meals provides great opportunities for children to exercise their finger muscles.
- Teach children how to tie their shoes.
- Place pompoms on the floor. Invite the children to take off their shoes and pick up the pompoms with their toes.
- Provide finger puppets that the children can use to tell stories from books or stories they make up.

Experiences and Activities for School-Age Children

- Encourage the children to use a computer keyboard. This is a great way to teach letter recognition and develop small muscles at the same time.
- Teach the children origami, the Japanese art of paper folding. There are several excellent books available with simple directions. Simple directions are also available on this website: www.tinyshiny.com/How-to_Projects.php.
- Teach the children how to crochet or knit and how to sew on buttons.
- Teach the children string tricks such as The Winking Eye and The Cup and Saucer. (Use a search engine to find directions for these string tricks and others.)
- Challenge the children to design and fold paper airplanes and then have a contest to find the plane that flies the longest distance.

- Use a deck of cards to teach the children simple magic tricks. (Use a search engine to find directions for simple card tricks.)

Ideas to Use with Two or More Children

- Teach children to play traditional games such as Jacks, Pickup Sticks, Marbles, Dominoes, Tiddlywinks, and Drop the Clothespin.
- Play Hot Potato. Gather the children in a circle. Pass a beanbag around the circle while music is playing. When the music stops, the child with the beanbag is out of the game. Continue until only one child is left. Invite children who are out of the game to clap as the remaining children pass the beanbag.

Books for Infants and Toddlers

Hand, Hand, Fingers, Thumb by Al Perkins
Ten Little Fingers and Ten Little Toes by Mem Fox
Ten Little Fingers by Annie Kubler
This Little Piggy by Annie Kubler

Books for Preschool Children

Busy Fingers by C.W. Bowie
Cleversticks by Bernard Ashley
Finger Rhymes by Marc Brown
Hand Rhymes by Marc Brown
Hand, Hand, Fingers, Thumb by Al Perkins
Harold and the Purple Crayon by Crockett Johnson
Here Are My Hands by Bill Martin Jr. and John Archambault
A Painter by Douglas Florian
The Paper Crane by Molly Bang

Books for School-Age Children

Art & Max by David Wiesner
Can You Hear It? by William Lach

Want to Read More?

Cabrera, D. & Cotosi, L. 2009. The world at our fingertips. *Scientific American Mind.* 21 (4): 49–55.

Jensen, E. 2008. *Brain-based learning: The new paradigm of teaching.* New York: Corwin Press.

Ratley, J. & Hagerman, E. 2008. *Spark: The revolutionary new science of exercise and the brain.* New York: Little, Brown and Company.

Calm, Cool, and Collected?

CHAPTER TWENTY-THREE

STRESS AND THE BRAIN

Stress can be dangerous to both the body and the brain. Stress stimulates the release of a chemical called cortisol into the brain. Cortisol (hydrocortisone) is a steroid hormone produced by the adrenal gland. Stress impairs the body's immune system. Prolonged stress can cause problems with memory, blood pressure, problem-solving capabilities, and thought processes. Prolonged stress in children can actually destroy fragile newly wired neurological connections (Shore, 2003).

Not all stress is bad. There are three variations in levels of stress:

1. Positive stress increases the heart rate and stimulates only mild elevations in stress hormone levels. A small amount of stress is not harmful to the brain. It actually acts as a motivator. A small amount of stress keeps arousal levels high and encourages the completion of a task.
2. Tolerable stress is serious but manageable. It causes temporary elevations in stress hormone levels, but these elevations can be buffered by supportive relationships.
3. Toxic stress creates prolonged activation of the stress response system. Coupled with the absence of protective relationships, it is extremely damaging to both physical health and brain function. Toxic stress levels impact the structure and capacity of the brain in children. Sources of toxic stress

STRESS CAN BE DANGEROUS TO BOTH THE BODY AND THE BRAIN.

153

include neglect, abuse, exposure to violence, homelessness, parental mental illness, parental incarceration, and other serious life situations.

Both short- and long-term stress impair memory. Stress, whether short- or long-term, causes the brain to age more quickly because of the cortisol released into it. The stress-related release of cortisol interferes with brain function by slowing down the neurotransmitter activity and increasing the release of glucose and calcium in the brain cells. Slower neurotransmitters mean slower processing of information. Some glucose is important, as glucose fuels the brain. But prolonged high levels glucose may exhaust brain cells and lead to fatigue. Higher levels of calcium create free-radical molecules, which can directly kill and damage brain cells. In order to slow down the brain's aging process and prevent the diminishment of memory functions, the brain requires time to relax, time when it is free from stress.

Although some stress is inevitable, research shows that stress can undermine the learning process. Stress disrupts working memory and reduces a person's desire to explore new ideas and creatively solve problems. While some children under stress will work "harder," the quality of the work decreases. Higher stress levels create greater negative impact, crippling short-term memory. In these situations, a child experiences difficulty retrieving previous information from memory. High stress levels also decrease a child's decision-making ability.

Emerging research (Korosi, et al., 2010; Maselko, et al., 2010) investigates how maternal care and love relate to the development of resilience. For example, if a child is in a stressful situation, the cortisol damage to brain structure and capacity is offset by his relationship with his mother. To put it simply, love is a great equalizer when it comes to stress damage—it reduces the long-term effects.

Ideas for Reducing Stress

Experiences and Activities for Infants and Toddlers

☐ Watch for signs of stress. These are often the same signs infants demonstrate when they are overstimulated. When infants arch their backs, pull away, turn their heads away, or cry, it indicates that they are stressed. When toddlers cry, turn away, or close their eyes, they are indicating they are stressed.

☐ Rock babies and sing them soft lullabies when they appear stressed.

☐ Hold a stressed baby close against your shoulder and make a soft swooshing sound close to the baby's ear.

☐ If children are not crying, allow them to rest in a quiet place.

☐ Keep noise levels down as much as possible around infants and toddlers.

Experiences and Activities for Preschool Children

☐ Discuss stress with children. Point out some of the causes of stress, such as adjusting to new places, people, or things; being tired or hungry; being in a rush; reacting to the stress of others; conflicts with others; and changes.

☐ Teach children calming strategies. Here is a list of a few strategies that work well with children:

  ▪ Bringing hands to the center of the body: Just as crossing the midline activates the brain, bringing hands to the midline calms the brain.

  ▪ Stretching: Encourage the children to stretch when they are feeling stressed. Teach them the following action rhyme they can sing to themselves when they stretch to relieve stress:

    Stretch to the Windows
    Stretch to the windows.
    Stretch to the door.
    Stretch to the ceiling.
    Stretch to the floor.

  ▪ Listening to relaxing music

  ▪ Breathing

  ▪ Making "Butterfly Wings": Hold arms beside the body. Lift arms overhead while inhaling deeply. Exhale, and bring arms back down beside the body.

  ▪ Exercising

  ▪ Releasing: Pretend to let the stress drain from your fingertips like rain from a cloud.

> HIGH STRESS LEVELS DECREASE A CHILD'S DECISION-MAKING ABILITY.

- Flopping: Teach the children the following action rhyme as a way to "flop" away stress:

Floppy Rag Doll (suit actions to words)
Flop your arms, flop your feet,
Let your hands go free.
You're the floppiest rag doll
I am ever going to see.

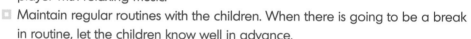

- Talking to a friend
- Taking imaginary trips:
  Pretend you are floating on a
  cloud over a beautiful ocean or
  swimming peacefully in a warm pond.
- Provide a quiet place children can go
  to when they feel stressed. Equip this
  area with stress balls, books, pillows, and a music
  player with relaxing music.
- Maintain regular routines with the children. When there is going to be a break in routine, let the children know well in advance.
- Sing with children. Singing increases endorphins, which reduce the release of cortisol.
- Use humor with children. Laughter reduces stress.
- Teach children to ask for and accept help from others. Teach children to give help when asked by modeling this behavior.
- Provide sensory activities for children. It can be calming to explore and play with water and sand.
- Go on "talk walks" with children. Go outside and walk in a familiar direction, then stop and encourage the children to enjoy the feel of the wind, the warmth of the sun, and the smell of nature.

Experiences and Activities for School-Age Children

- Encourage children to keep journals with descriptions of the times when they feel stressed. Help the children find patterns in the events that cause their stress, and challenge the children to think of ways they might make their lives less stressful.

- Ask children to make up stretching chants, and then recite the chants with the children while they stretch.
- Having too much to do can play a role in creating stress. Teach children how to create a to-do list. Point out how nice it feels to have a day's tasks organized, and how good it feels to check something off a to-do list.
- Talk with the children about how clutter can cause stress. Encourage children to keep their work spaces organized and uncluttered.
- Teach children yoga.

Ideas to Use with Two or More Children

- Have children select a friend to talk with each morning. Suggest that the children tell their friends about things they did the day before. This activity familiarizes children with the act of communicating about their lives and may prepare them to use this strategy when feeling stressed.
- Teach children how to give their friends neck massages or back rubs to help reduce stress.
- Encourage families to make sure that their children get enough sleep. Preschoolers need a combined total of 10 hours of sleep each day (between naps and nighttime sleep), and school-age children need eight hours each day.

A SMALL AMOUNT OF STRESS IS NOT HARMFUL TO THE BRAIN.

Book for Toddlers

The Monster at the End of This Book by Jon Stone

Books for Preschoolers

Alexander and the Terrible, Horrible, No Good, Very Bad Day by Judith Viorst
Strega Nona by Tomie dePaola

Books for School-Age Children

If I Were in Charge of the World and Other Worries by Judith Viorst

Learning to Slow Down and Pay Attention by Kathleen Nadeau

What to Do When You Worry Too Much: A Kid's Guide to Overcoming Anxiety by Dawn Huebner

Want to Read More?

Korosi, A. & Baram, T.Z. 2010. The pathways from mother's love to baby's future. http://academic.research.microsoft.com/Paper/13196882

Korosi, A. et al. 2010. Early life experience reduces excitation to stress-responsive hypothalamic neurons and reprograms the expression of corticotropin-releasing hormone. *The Journal of Neuroscience,* 30 (2): 703–713

Maselko J., Kubzansky L., Lipsitt L., & Buka S. L. 2010. Mother's affection at 8 months predicts emotional distress in adulthood. *Journal of Epidemiology and Community Health,* Online First, July 26, 2010.

Shore, R. 2003. *Rethinking the brain,* revised. Washington, DC: Families and Work Institute.

Sousa, D. 2005. *How the brain learns,* 3rd edition. New York: Corwin Press.

University of California, Irvine. 2008. Short-term stress can affect learning and memory. *Science Daily,* March 11.

The Good
The Bad, and
The Unknown

CHAPTER TWENTY-FOUR

TECHNOLOGY
AND THE BRAIN

Technology has both a positive and a negative impact on the brain. The brain's neural circuitry responds every moment to sensory input. This constant reshaping of our brain is referred to as *neural plasticity*. The explosion in technology (smart phones, computers, video games, and so on) is profoundly altering the evolution of our brains. These technologies are gradually strengthening new neural pathways in our brains and simultaneously weakening old pathways (Small & Vorgan, 2008).

> DIGITAL TECHNOLOGY IS NOT ONLY INFLUENCING HOW WE THINK BUT ALSO HOW WE FEEL.

On the positive side, technology is improving some cognitive abilities, including the ability to react more quickly to visual stimuli, and the skill of noticing images in peripheral vision.

On the negative side, technology is creating something identified by Linda Stone in 1998 as *continuous partial attention,* which means keeping tabs on many things while never truly focusing on any one thing. Hours of digital connectivity can create a unique type of brain strain, making people feel fatigued, irritable, and distracted.

Digital technology is not only influencing how we think but also how we feel. As the brain evolves and shifts its focus toward new technological skills, it drifts away from fundamental social skills (e.g., reading facial expressions, grasping the emotional context of a subtle gesture). A Stanford study found that for every hour we spend on our computers, video games, or television, traditional face-to-face interaction time with other people drops by thirty minutes. Researchers suggest that we are losing personal touch with our real-life relationships and may be developing an artificial sense of intimacy (Goleman, 2007).

Ideas for Using Technology to the Best Advantage of the Brain

Experiences and Activities for Infants and Toddlers

☐ Using technology is inappropriate for infants and toddlers. Children under two need to be spending time interacting with the people in their lives and with their environment. The American Academy of Pediatrics advises no screen time for children under the age of two. These early years are crucial in a child's development. The academy is concerned about the impact of computers and television programming during this crucial period. Any positive effect of screen time on infants and toddlers is still open to question, but the benefits of adult-child interactions are proven. For more information, visit www.aap.org.

☐ Use technology to help you learn songs and stories, and then spend time talking, singing, reading, listening to music, and playing with little ones.

> TECHNOLOGY HAS BOTH A POSITIVE AND A NEGATIVE IMPACT ON THE BRAIN.

Experiences and Activities for Preschool Children

☐ Limit use of technology for preschool children. Young children learn by doing (running, building with blocks, dressing up, playing house, working puzzles, exploring fingerpaints, and a multitude of other active activities). The National Association for the Education of Young Children (NAEYC) advises that "computers supplement, and do not replace, highly valued early childhood activities and materials, such as art, blocks, sand, water, books, exploration with writing materials, and dramatic play" (NAEYC,

1996). The Northwest Regional Education Laboratory recommends no more than two hours of screen time (computer, television, and video-game time combined) a day for preschoolers.

- To balance screen time:
  - Encourage children to have face-to-face interactions with peers.
  - Be fully present with children. Model paying close attention and responding sincerely when children are speaking.
- Watch television or videos with children. You can help the experience be more beneficial by asking questions that encourage children's thinking.
- Be selective about what you make available for children to watch on television, videos, or the computer. Many games and programs are inappropriate for younger children.

Experiences and Activities for School-Age Children
- Teach kids to be media savvy. Discuss the pros and cons of technology.
- Have children keep a log of the number of hours they spend involved in some form of technology (television, computers, video games, and so on), and then engage them in a discussion about when they use technology and how and why they use it.

Books for Preschool Children

Berenstain Bears and Too Much TV by Stan Berenstain and Jan Berenstain
The Boy with Square Eyes by Juliet and Charles Snape
Cam Jansen and the Mystery of the Television Dog by David Adler
Curious George series by H. A. Rey
Have You Filled Your Bucket Today? A Guide to Daily Happiness for Kids by Carol McCloud

Books for School-Age Children

The Boy Who Invented TV: The Story of Philo Farnsworth by Kathleen Krull
What Was It Like Before Television? by Rosie Hankin

Want to Read More?

Boyse, K. 2010. Television and children. *YourChild: Development and behavior besource.* University of Michigan Health Services: Ann Arbor. www.med.umich.edu/yourchild/topics/tv.htm.

Dixon, K. 2005. Researchers link use of Internet, social isolation. *Stanford University News.* February 23. http://news.stanford.edu/news/2005/february23/internet-022305.html.

Goleman, D. 2006. *Social intelligence: The new science of human relationships.* New York: Bantam Dell.

Goleman, D. 2007. Flame first, think later: New clues to e-mail misbehavior, *New York Times,* February 20, Health Section.

Nie, N. H. & Erbring, L. 2002. Internet and society: A preliminary report, *IT & Society* 1 (1): 275-83.

Roberts D. F., Foehr U.G., & Rideout, V. 2005. *Generation M: Media in the lives of 8–18-year-olds.* Report published by the Kaiser Family Foundation. www.kff.org/entmedia/upload/Generation-M-Media-in-the-Lives-of-8-18-Year-olds-Report.pdf.

Small, G. & Vorgan, G. 2008. *iBrain: Surviving the technological alteration of the modern mind.* New York: Collins Living.

Van Scoter, J., Ellis, D. & Railsback, J. 2001. Technology in early childhood education: Finding the balance. Northwest Educational Regional Laboratory. U.S. Dept. of Education, Office of Educational Research and Improvement.

NAEYC. 1996. Technology and young children: Ages 3 through 8. A position statement of the National Association for the Education of Young Children. http://www.naeyc.org/files/naeyc/file/positions/PSTECH98.PDF

Glossary

Adrenalin—A hormone released during times of stress.

Amygdala—A structure in the limbic region of the brain that encodes emotional messages to the hippocampus.

Auditory learning style—Learners use auditory stimuli, such as listening and speaking, to activate learning.

Autonomic nervous system—The involuntary system of nerves that controls and stimulates the output of two hormones, cortisol from the adrenal cortex and adrenalin from the adrenal medulla.

Axon—A long fiber that carries impulses from one neuron to the dendrites of other neurons.

Brain chemistry—The chemicals used by the brain for carrying messages from one neuron to another. Brain chemistry is responsible for our ability to speak, move, think, and feel.

Brain circuitry—An integrated system of neurological wiring that makes up the brain.

Brain-derived neurotrophic factor—A powerful protein produced by exercise that encourages brain cells to grow, interconnect, and communicate in new ways.

Brain research—A collection of scientific data related to brain development, function, and malfunction. In early childhood, the focus is often related to the development of brain structure, capacity, and function.

Brain stem—A seahorse-shaped part of the brain that receives sensory input from eleven of the body's twelve nerve endings. The brain stem also monitors our heartbeat, body temperature, and digestion.

Brain synapses—Connections between neurons from which information flows.

Cellular communication—Messaging passed chemically and by synapse from one cell to another.

Cerebellum—The part of the brain located at the base of the skull. It is responsible for muscle coordination and movement.

Cerebrum—The largest part of the brain. It controls speech, memory, sensory interpretation, and thinking.

Chemical balance—The state of optimum function that occurs when the hormones and chemicals that support neurotransmitters are in balance. An imbalance can lead to depression, anxiety, and reduced ability to think clearly. In some cases, imbalance is associated with mental illness.

Cognitive abilities—Mental processes such as thinking, perceiving, comparing, evaluating, and remembering.

Continuous partial attention—A term coined by Linda Stone in 1998 to describe the behavior of individuals who have developed the skill of keeping tabs on many things while never truly focusing on any one thing. Linda Stone believes this occurs when individuals spend too much time engrossed in digital technology.

Corpus callosum—A line of nerve cells connecting the left and right hemispheres of the brain.

Cortisol—A steroid hormone produced by the adrenal gland when one is stressed.

Dendrite—The branched formations from a neuron that receive impulses from other neurons through synaptic contact.

Digital technology—Electronic information that is presented in the form of discrete numeric symbols. It is not physical.

Dopamine—A neurotransmitter produced in the brain that is involved in movement and emotion as well as many brain activities.

EEG—An instrument that charts fluctuations in the brain's electrical activity.

Endorphins—Chemicals released by the pituitary gland and the hypothalamus when a person feels happy and excited. Endorphins produce a feeling of well-being.

Executive function—Mental processes that help individuals control and regulate abilities and behaviors.

Frontal cortex—The area of the brain just behind the forehead. This is the center of higher-level thought and reasoning.

Glial cells—Brain cells that surround each neuron for support, protection, and nourishment.

Hemisphere control—The ability to control automatic responses of the left or right hemisphere.

Hemisphere integration—The simultaneous use of both left and right hemispheres. Hemisphere integration occurs through the use of cells of the corpus callosum that make up the midline of the brain.

Hippocampus—The part of the brain that compares new learning to past learning and encodes information to long-term memory.

Hormones—Chemicals released by cells and glands. Hormones carry messages from one part of the body to another.

Imaging tools—Tools scientists use to study brain function, structure, and energy of the living brain. These instruments include Ultrasound, CAT, MRI, MEG, NIRS, fMRI, PET, and EEG.

Immune system—A complex system of cellular and molecular components having the primary function of providing defense against foreign organisms or substances.

Impulsivity—The inability to control one's impulses; the inability to act with forethought.

Interactive perspective—The view that brain structure is a result of a complex interplay between genes and the environment.

Interleukins—Proteins that direct other cells to divide and differentiate to boost the immune system.

Intrinsic motivation—The desire to begin or finish a task that originates from internal desires as opposed to external rewards.

Kinesthetic learning style—Learners use movement, such as clapping or note taking, to activate learning.

Lateralization—The tendency for each hemisphere of the brain to specialize in specific functions.

Limbic system—The portion of the brain that includes the hippocampus and amygdala. This is also where emotions are controlled.

Long-term memory—The storage of information for an indefinite period of time where it can be recalled as needed.

Meaning—The learner establishes "meaning" to new information when he or she determines its relevance and/or applies new information. Establishing meaning assists in the processing of information into long-term learning.

Memory—The ability to store and recall information.

Mirror neurons—Neurons assigned to wiring social reflections. Mirror neurons begin to wire at birth and continue to wire during the first two years of life. An individual's capacity for empathy is directly related to the number of mirror neurons wired.

MRI (Magnetic Resonance Imaging)—An instrument that uses radio waves to produce high-contrast images of internal structures.

Neural networks—An interconnected group of neurons that interact simultaneously and in interconnected combinations.

Neural plasticity—The ability of neural connections to reroute themselves up until the arrival of puberty.

Neurogenesis—The daily process by which the brain makes new neurons.

Neuron—The basic cell making up the brain and nervous system.

Neuroscience—Any of the sciences that deal with the study of the nervous system.

Neurotransmitter—Chemicals stored in an axon sac that are responsible for transmitting impulses from neuron to neuron across synaptic gaps.

Norepinephrine—A chemical that can be a hormone or a neurotransmitter. It is secreted into the blood by the adrenal medulla as a hormone, and from neurons as a neurotransmitter.

Nutrients—Chemical elements or compounds needed for growth and health.

Olfactory nerve—One of twelve cranial nerves. This nerve is responsible for the sense of smell and is the only nerve that goes unfiltered into the brain.

Perceptual register—A process in the brain stem that filters incoming stimuli before it is passed to working memory.

Perceptual-sensory—The process of becoming aware of and learning about the environment by applying sensory input.

Peripheral vision—The ability to see items that are outside one's direct line of vision. This is often referred to as "side vision."

PET (Positron Emission Tomography)—A scanner that traces the metabolism of radioactively tagged sugar in the brain tissue to produce imagery of cell activity.

Prefrontal cortex—The area of the brain at the front of the head just below the forehead. This area is responsible for executive function, mediating conflicting thoughts, regulating social interactions, and repressing emotions.

Primary olfactory cortex—The portion of the cortex involved in the sense of smell.

Prosody—The natural melody of speech created by rhythmic and intonational aspects of language.

RAS (Reticular Activating System)—A formation of neurons in the brain stem that channels sensory information through the perceptual register.

Replication—The brain's repetition of previously learned information and routine situations.

Resilience—The ability to bounce back from adversity and stress.

Retention—The preservation of information in long-term memory.

Sense—The learner makes sense of information by examining patterns and comparing past learning to the new. Information processing is dependent on the learner making sense of the information.

Sensory input—Information received from the senses (through nerve impulse) and directed to the brain, where it will be filtered or processed.

Serotonin—A neurotransmitter found in the central nervous system. Serotonin generally produces a sense of well-being.

Short-term memory—A temporary memory where information is processed briefly and unconsciously before being blocked or passed on to working memory.

Spindle cells—Neurons related to social judgment and sensitivity that begin to position themselves in the brain during the first four months of life. How prolific these neurons become is dependent on the environment. A kind, loving environment increases the number of neurons; whereas, a neglectful environment reduces the number of neurons.

Steroid hormone—Lipid molecules that act as hormones by causing chemical changes in body cells. They are synthesized and secreted into the bloodstream by endocrine glands such as the adrenal cortex and the gonads (ovary and testis). They are necessary for vital body functions including the production of anti-inflammatory agents and the regulation of events that occur during pregnancy.

Stress response system—When the body is stressed by trauma, illness, a threat, or any number of other challenges, the brain activates the autonomic nervous system, the involuntary system of nerves that controls and stimulates the output of two hormones, cortisol from the adrenal cortex and adrenalin from the adrenal medulla. These two hormones and the activity of the autonomic nervous system come to the rescue. The autonomic nervous system helps maintain alertness by increasing the heart rate and blood pressure and quickly marshalling energy reserves. Cortisol, on the other hand, works more slowly. It helps reload energy supplies and, at the same time, encourages memory of important information.

Surface tension—The property of a liquid to resist external force. For example, dewdrops on a blade of grass and foil floating on water are both examples of surface tension.

Synapse—A microscopic gap between the axon of one neuron and the dendrite of another.

Synaptic gaps—The space that exist between axons terminals and receiving dendrites where synapses occur.

Start Smart, Revised

Unconscious—A state of actions or movements that are implemented without awareness.

Visual learning style—Learners use visual images, such as story maps or book illustrations, to activate learning.

Windows of opportunity—Fertile times when the brain is particularly susceptible to specific types of wiring. Birth opens the windows, and puberty normally signals the time for the windows to close. Positive experiences result in positive outcomes. Negative experiences result in negative outcomes.

Working memory—Temporary memory where information is processed in the hippocampus. Space for temporary memory is limited. For information to be processed, the learner must make sense of the data and establish meaning.

Appendix

ADDITIONAL RESEARCH

Chapter 5
I Feel, I Remember: Emotions and the Brain

Mirror neurons allow us to mimic the feelings and movements of others. Babies demonstrate the wiring of mirror neurons when they smile back at us just a few short weeks after birth. We demonstrate our use of mirror neurons when we smile back at someone without even thinking or when we catch the "fever" of exhilaration of the crowd at a sports event. If we are upbeat and those around us are sullen and negative, we will likely follow suit in a short period of time.

Goleman, D. 2006. *Social intelligence: The new science of human relationships.* New York: Bantam Dell.

Chapter 6
Hop, Skip, Jump: Exercise and the Brain

Adrenaline heightens our perceptions, speeds up heart rates, and prepares our bodies for fight or flight. The chemical reactions that occur during exercise provide practice for the similar responses needed in challenging situations.

Exercise helps to stimulate neurogenesis by releasing special protein factors that encourage the brain's innate stem cells to divide. It also provides a healthier internal environment for the growth of new cells, which increases the chance that they can function as healthy nerve cells.

Ratley, J. & Hagerman, E. 2008. *Spark: The revolutionary new science of exercise and the brain.* New York: Little, Brown and Company.

Chapter 11
Touch, Toss, Turn, Twirl: Movement and the Brain

Based on research assembled over the last 15 years, it appears that hands-on explorations contribute not only to the understanding of abstract concepts but also to four critical-thinking skills essential to learning: making distinctions, recognizing relationships, organizing systems, and seeing things from multiple perspectives. This higher-level thinking starts with touch (Cabrera, 2010).

Cabrera, D. and Cotosi, L. 2009. The world at our fingertips. *Scientific American Mind.* 21 (4): 49–55.

Chapter 12
Start with a Song: Music and the Brain

"The neurological ties between music and language go both ways; a person's native tongue influences the way that person perceives music. The same progression of notes may sound different depending on the language the listener learned growing up. Speakers of tonal languages (most Asian languages) are much more likely than Westerners to have perfect pitch. All languages have a "melody" that is unique. Infants echo the inherent melodies of their native language when they cry, long before they speak."

Deutsch, D. 2010. Speaking in tunes. *Scientific American Mind.* 21 (3): 36–43.

Playing an instrument may help children better process speech in noisy classrooms, and more accurately interpret the nuances of language that are conveyed by subtle changes in the human voice. This information has implications for children with autism and auditory dyslexia.

Professional musicians put extraordinary effort into practicing their instruments. By the age of 21, it is estimated that professional musicians have played for 10,000 hours. Until recently, it was unclear what effect this experience has on the brains and behavior of musicians. Neuroscientists are studying musicians to assess how performing and practicing music alter psychophysics, cognition, and synaptic physiology. These studies explore the brain's experience-dependent plasticity. Researchers are studying how musical training influences the processing and perception of sound, and are also examining the effect of music education on brain development. Recent research indicates that musicians excel in areas other than musical ability. For example, they outclass most in processing speech and emotionally expressive sounds.

Parbery-Clark, A., Skoe, E., & Kraus, K. 2009. Music and the brain. *The Journal of Neuroscience* 29 (45): 14100–14107.

The term *Mozart effect* comes from several studies regarding the effect that listening to Mozart has on brain activity. In the original study (Leng & Shaw, 1990) participants demonstrated increased abilities in spatial learning, memory, and reasoning. In studies that included preschoolers and college students, the researchers found that the brain activity waves had remarkable similarities to the written score of Mozart-composed music. This test stirred interest in the academic community which motivated several other research teams to conduct similar experiments, with incongruent results.

In 1991, Shaw and Leng conducted another study on the effect of music on the brain. They found that nerve cells adopt certain specific firing patterns and rhythms. Shaw and Leng surmised that these patterns form the basic exchange of mental activity. They turned the output of their nerve cell simulations into sounds instead of a conventional printout. To their surprise, the rhythmic patterns sounded somewhat familiar, with some of the characteristics of baroque, new age, or Eastern music. They hypothesized that if brain activity can sound like music it might be possible to use the patterns in music to stimulate the brain.

Three years later Shaw joined other researchers in creating the study that coined the term *Mozart Effect*. They assigned 36 students to one of three groups. Group A listened to a selection by Mozart. Group B listened to a "relaxation tape," and Group C spent 10 minutes in silence. All participants then took a spatial IQ test. Group A averaged 9 points higher on the test. The increase was temporary, lasting for only 10 to 15 minutes. This test stirred enough interest in the academic community to induce several other research teams to conduct similar experiments, with disparate results (Rauscher, 1993).

Although these later studies do not refute that music has an influence on the brain, they do question whether or not music—by Mozart or by others—can help to raise an individual's IQ.

Leng, X. 1990. Investigation of higher brain functions in music composition using models of the cortex based on physical system analogies. PhD diss., University of California, Irvine.

Leng, X., Shaw, G. L., & Wright, E. L. 1990. Coding of musical structure and the trion model of cortex. *Music Perception*, 8: 49-62.

Leng, X., & Shaw, G. L. 1991. Toward a neural theory of higher brain function using music as a window. *Concepts in Neuroscience*, 2: 229–258.

Rauscher, F. H., Shaw, G. L., & Kn, K. N. 1993. Music and spatial task performance, *Nature* 365: 611.

Chapter 13
The Power of New: Novelty and the Brain

Some research studies examine why some individuals seek novelty even in the face of danger while others studiously withdraw. Although novelty-seeking has been determined to be primarily an aspect of personality, neuroscience is beginning to understand how the brain of a high-sensation seeker might be different from that of someone who generally avoids risk. Recent brain imaging studies have found a direct link between the size of the hippocampus and experience-seeking behavior which sheds light on how the brain responds differently to intense or arousing stimuli in highs vs. lows (Martin et al, 2007).

Martin, S.B., Covell, D.J., Joseph, J.E., Chebrolu, H., Smith, C.D., Kelly, T.H., Jiang, Y., & Gold, B.T. 2007. Human experience seeking correlates with hippocampus volume: convergent evidence from manual tracing and voxel-based morphometry. *Neuropsychologia 45,* 2874–2881.

Chapter 14

Feeding the Brain: Nutrition and the Brain

Although it is important for expectant mothers to eat nutritiously throughout pregnancy, it is particularly important between the tenth and eighteenth week of pregnancy when the baby's brain is growing rapidly. The brain experiences another growth spurt around age two. Malnutrition during these periods may have devastating effects on the nervous system. Malnutrition can affect both the growth of neurons and glial cells. Effects on glial cells may alter the development of myelination. In other words, it may limit the strength of neural connections (Dauncey, 2009).

Not all effects of poor diet are permanent. Some can be repaired by changing to a proper diet. Researchers believe that the timing of malnutrition is an important factor in determining the damage (Dauncey, 2009; Bedi, 2003).

Bedi, K.S. 2003. Nutritional effects on neuron numbers. *Nutrition Neuroscience.* 6 (3):141–52.
Dauncey, M.J. 2009. New insights into nutrition and cognitive neuroscience. *Proceedings of the Nutrition Society.* 68(4): 408–15.

Chapter 20

Spanish, Japanese, Vietnamese: Learning a Second Language and the Brain

Some social psychologists speculate that the brain changes caused by literacy may result in cultural differences in memory, attention, and visual perception. For example, John Gabrieli and a team of researchers from MIT report that European-Americans and students from several East Asian cultures show different patterns of brain activation when making snap judgments about visual patterns (Gabrieli et al., 2008).

Gabrieli, J., Hedden, T., Ketay, S., & Aron, A. 2008. Cultural influences in neural substrates of attentional control. *Psychological Science* 19(1): 12–17. Association for Psychological Sciences. Washington, DC.

Chapter 24

The Good, the Bad, and the Unknown: Technology and the Brain

As of October 26, 2009, television viewing among kids was at an eight-year high. On average, children ages two to five spend 32 hours a week in front of a television—watching television, DVDs, DVR and videos, and using a game console. Kids ages 6 to 11 spend about 28 hours a week in front of the television. The vast majority of this viewing (97 percent) is of live television.

Seventy-one percent of children from 8 to 18 years old have a television in their bedrooms; 54 percent have a DVD/VCR player, 37 percent have cable/satellite television, and 20 percent have premium channels.

McDonough, P. TV viewing among kids at an eight-year high. Nielsenwire. October 26, 2009. Available at: http://blog.nielsen.com/nielsenwire/media_entertainment/tv-viewing-among-kids-at-an-eight-year-high/.

Index

CHILDREN'S BOOK INDEX

A

A Fish Out of Water by Helen Palmer, 24

Abuela by Arthur Dorros, 138

Alexander and the Terrible, Horrible, No Good, Very Bad Day by Judith Viorst, 45, 47, 70, 157

Amazing Grace by Mary Hoffman, 45, 47, 79, 132

Amelia Bedelia Goes Camping by Peggy Parish, 54

Amos and Boris by William Steig, 144

Anna Banana: 101 Jump Rope Rhymes by Joanna Cole, 54

Apples and Pumpkins by Anne Rockwell, 144

Art and Max by David Wiesner, 152

B

Baby Dance by Ann Taylor, 47, 54, 79

Baby Danced the Polka by Karen Beaumont, 39

The Baby Dances by Katherine Henderson, 54, 144

Baby Faces by Margaret Miller, 47, 57, 126

The Belly Button Book by Sandra Boynton, 70

The Berenstain Bears and Too Much TV by Stan Berenstain, 161

Big Dog … Little Dog by P. D. Eastman, 112

The Birthday Ball by Lois Lowry, 86

Black on White by Tana Hoban, 29

A Book About Colors by Mark Gonyea, 29

Bored—Nothing to Do! by Peter Spier, 93

The Boy Who Invented TV: The Story of Philo Farnsworth by Kathleen Krull, 161

The Boy with Square Eyes by Juliet & Charles Snape, 161

Bread Is for Eating by David & Phyllis Gershator, 138

Bremen Town Musicians by various authors, 86

Brown Bear, Brown Bear, What Do You See? by Bill Martin Jr. & Eric Carle, 91, 109, 113

Busy Fingers by C. W. Bowie, 54, 152

C

The Cafeteria Lady from the Black Lagoon by Mike Thaler, 99

Calling Doctor Amelia Bedelia by Herman Parish, 113

Cam Jansen and the Mystery of the Television Dog by David Adler, 161

Can You Hear It? by William Lach, 152

Caps for Sale by Esphyr Slobodkina, 68, 113

The Care and Keeping of You: A Body Book for Girls by Valerie Schaefer, 24

Caritas by Todd Parr, 138

The Cat in the Hat by Dr. Seuss, 93

Celebrating Chinese New Year by Diane Hoyt-Goldsmith, 74

A Chair for My Mother by Vera B. Williams, 45, 47

A Chance for Esperanza by Pam Schiller, 138

Clap Your Hands by Lorinda Bryan Cauley, 39, 54

Clean Up Time by Elizabeth Verdick, 105

Cleversticks by Bernard Ashley, 152

A Color of His Own by Leo Lionni, 29

The Complete Book of Figure Skating by Carole Shulman, 40

A Cool Drink of Water by Barbara Kerley, 63

Cucu! by Roberta Grobel Intrater, 138

Curious George series by H. A. Rey, 161

D

D.W. the Picky Eater by Marc Brown, 99

Daddy Makes the Best Spaghetti by Anna Grossnickle Hines, 99

Dance by Bill T. Jones, 54

Dance Me, Daddy by Cindy Morgan, 144

Dance, Tanya by Patricia Lee Gauch, 39, 79, 132

The Dancing Dragon by Marcia K. Vaughan, 74

David Decides about Thumb Sucking by Susan M. Heitler, 24

David's Father by Robert Munsch, 122, 127

Diary of a Wimpy Kid series by Jeff Kinney, 24, 47, 70

A Dog's Purpose by Bruce Cameron, 113

Don't Be Afraid, Little Pip by Karma Wilson & Jane Chapman, 45

The Doorbell Rang by Pat Hutchins, 113, 127

Down by the Bay by Raffi, 86

Drinking Water by Mari C. Schuh, 63

A Drop of Water by Walter Wick, 63

Dulces Suenos: Sleep! by Roberta Grobel Intrater, 138

E

Eating the Rainbow by Rena Grossman, 99

Eight Animals Bake a Cake by Susanna Middleton Elya, 79

Emeka's Gift by Ifeoma Onyufulu, 138

Emma's Strange Pet by Jean Little, 132

Enemy Pie by Derek Munson, 79

Epossumondas by Coleen Salley, 113

Every Time I Climb a Tree by David McCord, 39

F

Falling Up by Shel Silverstein, 70, 93

Feelings by Joanne Murphy, 45, 47

Finger Rhymes by Marc Brown, 152

First Words by Louis Weber, 99

Fish Out of Water by Helen Palmer, 121

Five Little Monkeys Jumping on the Bed by Eileen Christelow, 113

Fortunately by Remy Charlip, 113

Frank Was a Monster Who Wanted to Dance by Keith Graves, 79

Frog and Toad series by Arnold Lobel, 113, 124

Frog Is Frightened by Max Velthuijs, 47

Froggie Went A-Courting by Chris Conover, 86

From Head to Toe by Eric Carle, 54

Funny Stories for 8 Year Olds by Helen Paiba, 70

G

Going Home by Eve Bunting, 45, 47

Goodnight Moon by Margaret Wise Brown, 112

Goodnight, Baby Bear by Frank Asch, 132

Green Eggs and Ham by Dr. Seuss, 96, 99

Growing Vegetable Soup by Lois Ehlert, 99

H

Hand Rhymes by Marc Brown, 39, 152

Hand, Hand, Fingers, Thumb by Al Perkins, 152

The Hardy Boys series by Franklin W. Dixon, 125

Harold and the Purple Crayon by Crockett Johnson, 152

Have You Filled Your Bucket Today? by Carol McCloud, 161

Have You Seen My Duckling? by Nancy Tafuri, 113

Head to Toe by Eric Carle, 79

Head, Shoulders, Knees and Toes by Annie Kubler, 79

Head, Shoulders, Knees, and Toes and Other Rhymes by Zita Newcome, 39

Henry and Mudge and the Tall Tree by Cynthia Rylant, 127

Here Are My Hands by Bill Martin Jr. & John Archambault, 144, 152

Hippos Go Berserk! by Sandra Boynton, 105

The Holes in Your Nose by Genichiro Yagyu, 144

How Do Dinosaurs Clean Their Rooms? by Jane Yolen, 118

I

I Am 3! Look What I Can Do! by Maria Carluccio, 118

I Can Share by Karen Katz, 132

I Hear by Helen Oxenbury, 74

I Like the Music by Leah Komaiko, 86

I Love Colors by Margaret Miller, 29

I See by Helen Oxenbury, 74

I Spy Treasure Hunt by Jean Marzollo, 118

I Touch by Helen Oxenbury, 74

I Was So Mad by Mercer Mayer, 24

If… by Sarah Perry, 93

If America Were a Village: A Book about the People of the United States by David J. Smith, 139

If I Were in Charge of the World and Other Worries by Judith Viorst, 158

Imogene's Antlers by David Small, 70, 93, 121–122, 127

Is It Red? Is It Yellow? Is It Blue? by Tana Hoban, 29

Itsy Bitsy Spider by Iza Trapani, 84, 86, 118

Ivy and Bean Doomed to Dance by Sophie Blackalll, 40

J

The Jazz Fly by Matthew Gollub, 86

Jenny's Hat by Ezra Jack Keats, 93

Jump, Frog, Jump by Robert Kalan, 113

Just a Mess by Mercer Mayer, 105

Just Like Daddy by Frank Asch, 132

K

Kids' Yoga Book of Feelings by Mary Humphrey, 106

The King Who Reigned by Fred Gwynne, 70

The Kissing Hand by Audrey Penn, 47, 144

L

Learning to Slow Down and Pay Attention by Kathleen Nadeau, 106, 158

Leo the Late Bloomer by Robert Kraus, 144

Listen to the Rain by Bill Martin Jr., 74

Little Bunny Follows His Nose by Katherine Howard, 20

The Little Red Hen by Byron Barton, 24

The Little Red Hen by Paul Galdone, 132

The Little Red Hen by various authors, 122, 127

Look, Look Again by Tana Hoban, 93

Love You Forever by Robert Munsch, 45, 47

Lullabies and Night Songs by William Engvick, 86

M

Madeleine by Ludwig Bemelmans, 138

Mama Zooms by Jane Cowen-Fletcher, 45, 47

Max Found Two Sticks by Brian Pinkney, 74, 118

Mealtime by Anthony Lewis, 99

Mike Mulligan and His Steam Shovel by Virginia Lee Burton, 127

Miss Mary Mack by Mary Ann Hoberman, 57

Moira's Birthday by Robert Munsch, 68, 105, 121, 127

The Monster at the End of this Book by Jon Stone, 157

More, More, More Said the Baby by Vera Williams, 24

Muddle Cuddle by Laurel Dee Gugler, 70

My Dog's Brain by Stephen Huneck, 58

My Many Colored Days by Dr. Seuss, 29

My Water Comes from the Mountain by Tiffany Fourmont, 63

N

Nancy Drew series by Carolyn Keene, 125

Nate the Great and the Big Sniff by Marjorie Weinman Sharmat, 20

Nate the Great by Marjorie Weinman Sharmat, 124, 127

No, No, Yes, Yes by Leslie Patricelli, 132

Noisy Nora by Rosemary Wells, 105

Nose Book by Al Perkins, 20

The Nose Knows by Avery Gilbert, 20

Now I Will Never Leave the Dinner Table by Jane Read Martin & Patrick Mark, 99

O

Old MacDonald Had a Farm by Robert M. Quackenbush, 86

Once upon MacDonald's Farm by Stephen Gammel, 68

Opposites by Sandra Boynton, 24, 112

Owl Babies by Martin Waddell, 45, 47

Owl Moon by Martin Waddell, 45, 47

P

A Painter by Douglas Florian, 152

The Paper Crane by Molly Bang, 152

The Park Bench by Fumiko Takeshita, 138

Peek-a-Boo by Francesca Ferri, 70

Peep-a-Who by Nina Laden, 92

Peter's Chair by Ezra Jack Keats, 24

Picasso by Mike Venezia, 29

Pocket Frog by Annie Kubler, 92

Q

Quiet Loud by Leslie Patricelle, 24

R

Ramona and Beezus by Beverly Cleary, 70

Ramona Quimby, Age 8 by Beverly Cleary, 24, 132

Ramona the Pest by Beverly Cleary, 47

Red Is Best by Kathy Stinson, 29

Rise Up Singing by Peter Blood & Annie Patterson, 43

Rosie's Walk by Pat Hutchins, 113

Run, Jump, Whiz, Splash by Very Rosenberry, 54

S

Schoolyard Rhymes: Kids' Own Rhymes for Rope-Skipping, Hand-Clapping, Ball-Bouncing, and Just Plain Fun by Judy Sierra & Melissa Sweet, 40

Shake It to the One You Love the Best by Cheryl Warren Mattox, 54

Silly Sally by Audrey Wood, 70, 74

Skates by Ezra Jack Keats, 39

Smell by Kay Woodward, 20

Smelling by Richard L. Allington, 20

Smelling Things by Allen Fowler, 20

Sniff, Sniff: A Book About Smell by Dana Meachen, 20

Sniffing and Smelling by Henry Arthur Pluckrose, 20

Something Special by Nicola Moon, 144

Song and Dance Man by Karen Ackerman, 39

Splash! by Roberta Grobel Intrater, 63

Stink and the World's Worse Super-Stinky Sneakers by Megan McDonald, 20

Stone Soup by Marcia Brown, 121, 127

Strega Nona by Tomie dePaola, 91, 157

Swimmy by Leo Lionni, 121, 127

T

Ten Black Dots by Donald Crews, 57, 74

Ten Little Fingers and Ten Little Toes by Mem Fox, 152

Ten Little Fingers by Annie Kubler, 152

The Tenth Good Thing About Barney by Judith Viorst, 45

This Isn't What It Looks Like by Pseudonymous Bosch, 93

This Little Piggy by Annie Kubler, 152

This Tree Is Older Than You by Naomi Shihab Nye, 139

Thomas' Snowsuit by Robert Munsch, 68

The Three Billy Goats Gruff by Paul Galdone, 121, 127

The Three Billy Goats Gruff by various authors, 24, 142

The Three Little Pigs by various authors, 24, 109

To Be a Kid by Maya Aimera, 54

Too Many Toys by David Shannon, 105

Too Much Noise by Ann McGovern, 105

The True Story of the Three Little Pigs by Jon Scieszca, 58

Tuesday by David Wiesner, 93

Twinkle, Twinkle, Little Star by Iza Trapani, 57, 86

V

The Very Busy Spider by Eric Carle, 113

The Very Hungry Caterpillar by Eric Carle, 91, 113

W

Wacky Wednesday by Theodore LeSieg, 68, 91, 93

Water by J. M. Parramon, 63

Water Is Wet by Penny Pollock, 63

The Water's Journey by Eleanor Schmid, 63

We're Going on a Bear Hunt by Michael Rosen, 113

What Was It Like Before Television? by Rosie Hankin, 161

The Wheels on the Bus by Raffi, 84, 86

When I Was Five by Arthur Howard, 118

Where Does Your Food Go? by Wiley Blivens, 99

Where Is Baby's Belly Button? by Karen Kratz, 70

Where Is My Baby? by Harriet Ziefert, 126

Where Is My Friend? by Simms Taback, 127

Where Is My House? by Simms Taback, 127

Where the Sidewalk Ends by Shel Silverstein, 70, 93

Whistle for Willie by Ezra Jack Keats, 118, 132

Who Said Moo? by Harriet Ziefert, 127

Y

You Read to Me, I'll Read to You by Mary Ann Hoberman, 144

Yummy Yucky by Leslie Patricelle, 24, 99

Z

Zin! Zin! Zin! A Violin by Lloyd Moss, 86

INDEX

A

Abdel-Azim, E., 70

Abstract concepts, 170

Abuse, 154

Adderall, 50

Adrenaline, 41, 50, 161, 163, 169

Alertness. *See* Mental alertness

Alike/different, 108

Allergies, 15–16, 96, 98, 151

Amabile, T., 132

American Academy of Pediatrics, 160

American Sign Language, 138, 146

Amygdala, 163

Analytical thinking, 55–56

Anderson, A., 87

Anxiety

aromas and, 15

color and, 25–26

Appetite

color and, 26, 28

Aroma, 15–20

alertness and, 17–19

attention and, 16–20

books about, 20

infants & toddlers, 16–17

memory and, 16, 19–20

preschool children, 17–19
   school-age children, 19–20
Aron, A., 139, 173
Asher, J. J., 139
Atonomic nervous system, 163
Attachment, 8, 10
Attention, 159, 161, 173
   aroma and, 16–20
   color and, 25–26, 28
   dehydration and, 59
   emotions and, 42
   nutrition and, 98
Attention-deficit hyperactivity
   disorder, 49–50
Auditory dyslexia, 170
Auditory learning styles, 71, 163
Autism, 170
Axon, 163

B
Baker, S. A., 133, 139
Balls, 38–39, 51–53, 76, 78, 85,
   120
Baram, T., 158
Barkovich, A. J., 15, 40
Bass, K. E., 82, 87
Batmanghelidj, F., 64
Beanbags, 19, 85, 152
Bedi, K. S., 100, 173
Berens, M. S., 139
Beyerstein, B. L., 74
Bicycles, 51, 90
Blankets, 66, 77
Bloch, C., 133, 139
Blocks, 61, 72–73, 91, 120, 124,
   160
Boas, D. A., 139
Body language, 55, 57

Books
   Learning to Slow Down and Pay
     Attention by Kathleen
     Nadeau, 106, 158
   Simple Signs by Carol
     Garboden Murray, 146

What to Do When You Worry
Too Much: A Kid's Guide to
Overcoming Anxiety by Bonnie
   Matthews, 158
What Was It Like Before
Television? by Rosie Hankin, 161
Bortfield, H., 133, 139
Boxes, 69, 147
Boyse, K., 161
Brackett, M. A., 48
Brain chemistry, 163
Brain circuitry, 163
Brain development
   aroma and, 15–20
   choices and, 21–24, 50, 104,
     131
   color and, 25–29, 110–111
   cross-lateral movement and,
     31–40, 56, 76, 79
   emotional intelligence and, 8–
     10, 41–48, 57, 65–70, 81–
     82, 169
   encouragement and, 129–132
   exercise and, 49–54, 75–80,
     169–170
   humor and, 46, 156
   hydration and, 59–64
   key findings, 8–11
   language skills and, 8, 22, 55–
     56, 133–140, 170–171
   laughter and, 65–70, 165
   learning styles and, 71–74
   meaning and, 165
   memory and, 41–48
   motor development and, 8, 10,
     31–40, 49–54, 75–80, 112,
     145–152, 160, 170
   music and, 81–87
   novelty and, 89–93, 172
   nutrition and, 8, 13, 95–100,
     172–173
   overstimulation and, 101–106,
     155
   patterns and, 12, 23, 83, 89,
     107–113, 115–119, 141,
     171

   problem solving and, 10, 43,
     46, 119–127, 153
   research into, 7–8
   second-language learning and,
     133–140, 173
   sense and meaning, 141–143
   small motor skills and, 145–152
   stress and, 9, 15, 25, 45, 49,
     65–66, 69, 153–158,
     173–174
   technology and, 159–162
   windows of opportunity, 9–10
Brain functions, 12–13
Brain hemispheres, 12, 55–58, 76,
   79, 120
   control and, 38, 164
   cross-lateral movement and,
     31–40
   infants, 56
   integration and, 164–165
   preschool children, 56–57
   toddlers, 56
Brain stem, 163
Brain synapses, 163
Brain teasers, 124
Brain-derived neurotrophic factor,
   163
Brainstorming, 28, 121
Brigance Diagnostic Inventory of
   Early Development, 116
Bubbles, 50, 77
Buka, S. L., 158
Buttons, 149–151

C
Cabrera, D., 145, 152, 170
Caceda, R., 47

Calming, 155
   aroma and, 15, 19
   color and, 25–26
Carey, B., 127
Cartoons, 69, 92
CAT scans, 11, 165
Cause and effect, 10, 55, 108, 110,
   120

Cellular communication, 163
Cerebellum, 163
Cerebrum, 163
Chebrolu, H., 93, 172
Chemical balance, 164
Chemical smells, 15
Choices, 21–23, 131
  books about, 24
  consumer, 23
  exercise and, 50
  increasing motivation, 22–23
  infants & toddlers, 22
  limiting, 22, 102, 104
  preschool children, 22–23
  school-age children, 23
  suggesting, 22
  with two or more children, 23
Choke testers, 146
Choking hazards, 96, 146
Christophe, A., 133, 139
Chudler, E., 70
Clapping, 110, 148–149
Classification, 116
Clean-up time, 151
Clutter, 104, 157
Cognitive abilities, 8, 22, 163
  brain hemispheres, 55–58
  emotions and, 47
  exercise and, 50
  practice and, 116
  small motor skills and, 145–152
  stress and, 153
  window of opportunity, 10
Cognitive delay, 49
Color, 25–29, 110–111
  books about, 29
  infants & toddlers, 26–27
  preschool children, 27
  school-age children, 27–28
  with two or more children, 28
Comparing, 57
Computers, 159–161
  keyboards, 151
Concrete examples, 56, 73
Conflicting messages, 57
Consequences, 22–23, 50, 125

Containers, 16–18, 150
"Continuous partial attention,"
  159, 163
Cooking activities, 17–19, 97–99,
  151
Cooperation, 10, 22, 52, 118
Coordination, 52–53, 77
Corpus callosum, 164
Cortisol, 164, 173–174
Cotosi, L., 152, 170
Counting skills, 61, 77
Covell, D. J., 93, 173
Cozolino, L., 47
Crawling, 32, 36, 77
Crayons, 35, 38, 90, 124
  scented, 19
Creativity
  color and, 26, 28
  exercise and, 50
Critical thinking skills, 145, 170
Crook, M. D., 82, 87
Cross-lateral movement, 31–40, 75
  infants & toddlers, 32, 56
  preschool children, 32–37, 76
  school-age children, 38, 79
  with two or more children,
    38–39
Crying, 155
Cups, 20, 61–63, 92, 124

D
da Vinci, Leonardo, 7
Daily routines, 91, 103, 111, 117,
  156
Dancing, 34–35, 39, 51, 79, 83,
  85, 110
Darwin, K. E., 24
Dauncey, M. J., 100, 173
Decision-making skills, 23, 42
  stress and, 154
Dehydration, 59–64
Delaying gratification, 50
Dendrite, 164
Dennison, G., 31, 40
Dennison, P., 31, 40

Depression
  aroma and, 15
  laughter and, 66
Descriptive language, 20, 28, 28,
  32, 42–43, 46, 57
Determination, 117
Deutsch, D., 81, 87, 170–171
Dewey, A., 54
Diffuse processing, 55
Digital technology, 164
Divergent processing, 55
Dixon, K., 162
Dolan, R. J., 20
Dopamine, 164
Dramatic play, 47, 57, 73, 84
Dramatic play center, 28
Dreams, 55
Drug abuse, 9
Düzel, E., 93

E
Early sounds, 10
EEGs, 11, 164–165
Ellis, D., 162
Emotional intelligence, 8–9, 41–48,
  57, 169
  infants & toddlers, 42, 66
  laughter and, 65–70
  music and, 82
  preschool children, 42–46,
    67–69
  prosody and, 81
  school-age children, 46, 69
  window of opportunity, 10
  with two or more children, 47
Empathy, 9
Encouragement, 129–132
  infants & toddlers, 130
  preschool children, 130–132
  school-age children, 132
Endorphins, 164
Energy
  aroma and, 15
  color and, 25
Engen, T., 16, 20
Environment, 8, 13, 116

Environmental feedback. *See* Feedback
Erbring, L., 162
Executive function, 164
Exercise, 49–54, 75–80, 169–170
    cross-lateral movement and, 31–40
    hydration and, 59
    infants & toddlers, 50–51, 76–77
    preschool children, 51, 78
    school-age children, 52, 79
    with two or more children, 52–53, 79
Exposure to violence, 154

F

Facial expressions, 42, 55, 57, 160
Fatigue
    aroma and, 15
    color and, 25–26
Feedback, 115–117, 129–132
Field trips, 124
    grocery, 98
    gym, 52
    high school concerts, 84–85
    opera, 84
    symphony, 84
Fight-or-flight response, 41, 50, 161
Finger paint, 76, 159, 161
Fingerplays
    "Open, Shut Them," 147
    "Ten Little Fingers," 147
Flowers, 19–20, 28
fMRIs, 11, 165
Foehr, U. G., 162
Following directions, 71
Franceschini, R., 139
Fraser, M. W., 24
Friederici, A. D., 133, 139
Friedrich, M., 133, 139
Frontal cortex, 164
Fruit juices, 19, 59–61
    frozen concentrate, 98
Fruits, 96, 98, 151
    dried, 96

G

Gabrieli, J., 139, 173
Gak recipe, 150
Galinsky, M. J., 24
Games, 46, 116, 136
    Animal Antics, 51
    Badminton, 79
    Cat and Mouse, 51
    Cooperative Musical Chairs, 112
    Dominoes, 152
    Drop the Clothespin, 152
    Duck, Duck, Goose, 92, 112
    Hello! My Name Is Joe! 77–78
    Hide and Seek, 112
    Horseshoes, 38–39
    Hot Potato, 152
    Jacks, 152
    Keep Away, 38
    Left Shoulder, Right Shoulder, 52
    Let's Pretend, 36
    Little Snail, 136–137
    Marbles, 152
    Miss Mary Mack, 147–149
    Mother, May I? 79
    Musical Ball Pass, 85
    Musical Chairs, 112
    Musical Freeze, 50–51
    Musical Hide and Seek, 85
    Parachute, 52–53
    Pat-a-Cake, 146
    Peekaboo, 66
    Pick-Up Sticks, 152
    Ping-Pong, 79
    Red Light, Green Light, 79
    'Round the House, 66, 136
    Simon Says, 92
    This Little Piggy, 146
    Tiddly Winks, 152
    Wall Ball, 38–39
    Washington Square, 66
    Who Stole the Cookie from the Cookie Jar? 149
    Word Scrabbles, 92
    You Can't Make Me Laugh," 69

Gardening activities, 19, 62, 98
Gardner, H., 108
Gelatin, 16, 19, 98
    shapes, 98
Gestures, 76, 78, 160
Gilkey, R., 47
Glial cells, 164, 173
Gold, B. T., 93, 172
Goldin-Meadow, S., 76, 80
Goleman, D., 8–9, 14, 42, 48, 160, 162, 169
Golinkoff, R., 106
Goop recipe, 150
Gordon, E., 8, 14
Gottfrield, J. A., 20
Graphing activities, 97
Greicius, M., 70

H

Hagerman, E., 49–50, 54, 80, 145, 151, 169
Haller, S., 139
Hand dominance, 35, 56
Hand-eye coordination, 23, 145–152
Hannaford, C., 32, 40, 54, 80, 120, 127
Hearing skills, 10, 12
    window of opportunity, 10
Hedden, T., 139, 173
Hernandez, A. E., 133, 139
Herz, R. S., 16, 20
Heslet, L., 87
Hill, Bonnie Campbell, 116
Hippocampus, 165, 172
Hirsh-Pasek, K., 106
Holistic thinking, 55
Homelessness, 154
Home-school connections, 143
Hotz, R. L., 134, 139
Humor, 46, 65–70, 90, 156
    immune system and, 65–69
    infants & toddlers, 66
    memory and, 65–69
    preschool children, 67–69
    school-age children, 69

with two or more children, 69
Hydration, 59–64
  infants & toddlers, 60
  preschool children, 60–62
  school-age children, 62–63
  with two or more children, 63

I
Imagery, 57
Imaging tools, 11, 165
Immune system
  defined, 165
  laughter and, 65–69
  stress and, 153
Impulsivity
  control, 10
  defined, 165
  exercise and, 50
Independence, 10
Infants
  aroma and, 16–17
  brain hemispheres, 56
  choices and, 22
  color and, 26–27
  cross-lateral movement, 32, 56
  encouragement and, 130
  hydration, 60
  laughter and, 66
  learning styles, 72
  long-term memory, 142
  motor development, 50–51,
    76–77
  music and, 82–83
  novelty and, 90
  nutrition and, 96
  overstimulation and, 103
  patterns and, 108
  practice and, 116
  problem solving and, 120
  second–anguage learning,
    133–140
  small motor skills, 146
  stress and, 155
  technology and, 160
Interactive-perspective, 8, 165
Interluekins, 165

Intrinsic motivation, 165
Intuitive thinking, 55, 57
Irritability
  aroma and, 15

J
Jensen, E., 24, 29, 42, 48, 65, 70,
  74, 115, 118–119, 127, 129,
  132, 145, 152
Jiang, Y., 93, 173
Jin Zhen, T., 140
Jonassen, D. H., 144
Joseph, J. E., 89, 93, 172
Journaling, 73, 156
Joy, 42–43, 46

K
Kaiser, A., 139
Kelly, T. H., 93, 172
Ketay, S., 139, 173
Kilts, C., 47
Kinesthetic learning style, 72, 165
Kjos, B. O., 15, 40
Kohn, A., 130, 132
Korosi, A., 154, 158
Kovelman, I., 139
Kraus, K., 87, 172
Kubzansky, L., 158
Kuenzli, E., 139
Kuwana, E., 70
Ky, K. N., 87, 172

L
Lam, C., 87
Land, S. M., 144
Language skills, 8, 22, 55–56,
  133–140, 170–171
  books about, 140
  infants & toddlers, 134–137
  preschool, 137
  school-age children, 138
  window of opportunity, 10
  with two or more children, 138
Lateralization, 55, 165
Laughter, 65–70, 165
  books about, 70

alertness and, 65
depression and, 66
immune system and, 65–69
infants & toddlers, 66
memory and, 65
memory and, 65–69
preschool children, 67–69
school-age children, 69
stress reduction, 65–66, 69
with two or more children, 69
Learning continuums, 116
Learning styles, 71–74, 165
  auditory, 71
  infants & toddlers, 72
  kinesthetic, 72
  preschool children, 72–73
  school-age children, 73
  visual, 71–72
  with two or more children,
    73–74
LeBoutillier, N., 54
Lemons, M., 8, 14
Leng, X, 82, 87, 171–172
Leon, M., 20
Levintin, D. J., 87
Li, H., 140
Li, P., 133, 139
Lieberman, H. R., 64
Limbic system, 165
  aroma and, 16
Linear processing, 55
Lipsitt, L., 158
Liu, X., 93
Logic, 42, 55, 57
Long–term memory, 13, 141–143
  defined, 165
  emotion and, 41
  infants & toddlers, 142
  patterns and, 107
  preschool children, 142–143
  school-age children, 144
Lowery, S., 54
Lynam, D., 93
Lynn, S. J., 74

M

Making distinctions, 145, 170
Mandel, D. R., 24
Martin, S. B., 93, 172
Maselko, J., 154, 158
Masking tape, 35, 123, 149
Maslow, A., 11
Matching skills, 19
Math skills, 55–56
Mathers, J. C., 100
Mayer, J., 48
McDonough, P., 162
McGaugh, J. L., 20
Meals, 22, 32, 59–60, 90–91, 95–100, 111, 146, 151
Meaning, 141–144, 165
  infants & toddlers, 142
  preschool children, 142–143
  school-age children, 144
Mednick, S., 127
MEGs, 11, 165
Memory, 41–48, 102, 171, 173–174
  aroma and, 16, 19–20
  defined, 165
  forming, 16
  infants & toddlers, 42
  laughter and, 65
  long-term, 13, 41, 107, 141–143
  music and, 82
  novelty and, 89–93
  practice and, 115
  preschool children, 42–46
  retention, 13
  school-age children, 46
  short-term, 12–13, 16, 50, 59, 157
  stress and, 153–154
  with two or more children, 47
Menon, V., 70
Mental alertness, 154
  aroma and, 15, 17–19
  color and, 26
  emotions and, 42
  hydration and, 59

  laughter and, 65
  novelty and, 89–93
  nutrition and, 98
  small motor skills and, 145
Miro, Joan, 28
Mirror neurons, 9, 165–166, 169
Mobbs, D., 70
Modeling, 23, 51, 84, 96, 116, 124, 156, 161
Mohiuddin, S., 87
Mondrian, Piet, 28
Mood
  color and, 25, 27–28
Moss, T., 54
Motivation
  emotions and, 41–42
  increasing, 22–23
  learning styles, 72
Motor control, 75–76
Motor development, 8, 49–54, 75–80, 112, 160, 170
  Cross-lateral movement, 31–40
  infants & toddlers, 50–51, 76–77
  preschool children, 51, 77–78
  school-age children, 52, 79
  small, 96–97, 110, 145–152
  window of opportunity, 10
  with two or more children, 52–53, 79
Mozart effect, 82, 171
Mozart, Wolfgang Amadeus, 7, 82, 84, 171
MRIs, 11, 165–166
Multiple intelligences, 12, 108
Multiple perspectives, 145–146, 170
Music, 9, 51, 55, 81–87, 108, 111, 170–171
  infants & toddlers, 82–83
  language development, 81–82
  preschool children, 83–84
  school-age children, 84–85
  with two or more children, 85–86
Musical instruments, 71, 170

  making, 83

N

Nash, J. K., 24
National Association for the Education of Young Children, 160–161
National Institute on Aging, 76
Neglect, 9, 154
Neural networks, 11–12, 166
Neural plasticity, 166
Neurogenesis, 166, 169
Neurons, 166, 173
Neuroscience, 11–14, 166, 170, 172
  brain functions, 12–13
  neural networks, 11–12
Neurotransmitters, 166, 174
Nie, N. H., 162
NIRSs, 11, 165
Non-linear development, 9
Non-responsive care, 9
Norepinephrine, 166
Northwest Regional Education Laboratory, 161
Novelty, 89–93, 172
  infants & toddlers, 90
  preschool children, 90–91
  school-age children, 91–92
  with two or more children, 92
Nutrition, 8, 13, 95–100, 172–173
  infants & toddlers, 96
  preschool children, 96–98
  school-age children, 98–99
  with two or more children, 99

O

Organizing systems, 145, 170
Outdoor activities, 35, 38, 51, 78, 91, 110–111, 156
Overstimulation, 101–106, 155
  infants & toddlers, 103
  preschool children, 103–104
  school-age children, 104
  signs of, 103
  with two or more children, 105

P

Parbery-Clark, A., 87, 170, 172
"Parentese," 81–82
Patience, 117
Patterns, 12, 23, 83, 89, 107–113, 116, 119, 141, 171
  infants & toddlers, 108
  preschool children, 108–111
  school-age children, 111
  with two or more children, 111–112
Peer teaching, 117–118, 144
Perry, B., 113
Persistence, 117–118
Petitto, L. A., 139
PETs, 11, 165–166
Physical development. *See* Motor development
Piaget, J., 11
Positive feelings
  cognitive skills and, 41–42
  color and, 25–26
  novelty and, 89, 91
Practice, 115–118
  infants & toddlers, 116
  preschool children, 116–117
  school-age children, 117
  with two or more children, 118
Praise, 129–132
  infants & toddlers, 130
  preschool children, 130–132
  school-age children, 132
Prefrontal cortex, 166
Preschool children
  aroma and, 17–19
  brain hemispheres, 56–57
  choices and, 22–23
  color and, 27
  cross-lateral movement, 32–37, 76
  emotions and, 57
  encouragement and, 130–132
  hydration and, 60–62
  laughter and, 67–69
  learning styles, 72–73
  long-term memory, 142–143

motor development, 51, 77–78
music and, 83–84
novelty and, 90–91
nutrition and, 96–98
overstimulation and, 103–104
patterns and, 108–111
practice and, 116–117
problem solving and, 121–125
second-language learning, 137
small motor skills, 147–151
stress and, 155–156
technology and, 160–161
Primary olfactory cortex, 167
Problem solving, 10, 43, 46, 119–127
  brain hemisphere, 56
  exercise and, 50
  infants & toddlers, 120
  preschool children, 121–125
  school-age children, 125–126
  stress and, 153
  with two or more children, 126
Provine, R. R., 70
Puzzles, 23, 69, 72, 84, 90, 111, 118, 143, 147, 160

R

Ramey, C., 11, 14, 16, 20, 26, 29, 42, 48
Ramey, S., 11, 14, 16, 20, 26, 29, 42, 48
Ratey, J., 49–50, 54, 75, 80, 145, 152, 169
Rauscher, F. H., 87, 171–172
Reasoning skills, 42, 55, 171
Recipes
  cinnamon rolls, 17
  creamy orange shakes, 99
  gak, 150
  gelatin playdough, 16
  gelatin shapes, 98
  goop, 150
  Kool-Aid playdough, 17–18
  letter pretzels, 97
  scented playdough, 17–18
Reflective questions, 143

Reiss, A., 70
Relationships, 12
  recognizing, 145, 170
  stress and, 153–154
  technology and, 159–160
Relaxation
  aroma and, 15, 19
  color and, 26
  learning, 45
Resilience, 167
Responsive care, 9, 13, 42
Retention, 167
Rewards, 129–132
  infants & toddlers, 130
  preschool children, 130–132
  school-age children, 132
Rhymes
  "Benjamin Franklin Went to France," 53
  "Come Right In," 53
  "Floppy Rag Doll," 156
  "Mable, Mable, See the Table," 53
  "Skipping to Town," 53
  "Stretch to the Windows," 155
Rhythm, 75, 81, 83, 171
Rideout, V., 162
Roberts, D. J., 162
Rocking, 77, 155
Role play, 47, 72–73, 91
Rugg, M. D., 20
Ruscio, J., 74

S

Sadness, 43
Salovey, P., 48
School-age children
  aroma and, 19–20
  choices and, 23
  color and, 27–28
  cross-lateral movement, 38, 79
  emotions and, 46
  encouragement and, 132
  hydration and, 62–63
  laughter and, 69
  learning styles, 73